Praise for Nail You~

"I was so impressed with *Nail Your Next Audition* that I gave several of the exercises to students who had juries coming up. It made a tremendous difference in their performances. This book is a "must-have" for young singers." **Vinson Cole, Professor of Voice and Tenor: MET, Paris Opera, Vienna, La Scala, San Francisco Opera, Seattle Opera Chicago Lyric Opera**

"Janet, I read the book. I think you've nailed it!!! You have nailed what's universal about the audition experience and should apply to any singer seeking to walk into a room, size it up, and go for it, with the right dosage of performance vis a vis concert presentation." **Christine Bullin, Former Director: Paris Opera Training Center, San Francisco Opera Center**

"I am one of those rare singers who loves to audition. In reading *Nail Your Next Audition*, I was shocked to see what I've been doing all these years to enjoy myself, brilliantly and succinctly written down! The next time I am asked my secret, I plan to say with insouciance: oh, check out that new book by Janet Williams on auditioning." **Steven Cole, Tenor: Salzburg Festival, Liceu Barcelona, Paris Opera, MET, San Francisco Opera, Chicago Lyric Opera**

"In the world of vocal training the subject of audition techniques is rarely addressed in such intricate detail as in *Nail Your Next Audition*. This book contains concepts that are extremely important to any young singer's training and can be very useful for the seasoned performer as well." **David L. Jones, International Vocal Pedagogue: New York, San Francisco, Paris, London, Berlin, Geneva, Amsterdam, Reykjavik**

Nail Your Next Audition

"Your book made so clear to me what was really lacking in my "package. I made a commitment to practice creative visualization daily, and I'm already seeing the results. I had a huge vocal breakthrough last week, just before recording a new demo." **Daniel Gundlach, Counter-Tenor: Paris Opera, Chicago Lyric Opera, New York City Opera**

"Your book is amazing! As a teacher of singing, manager and international opera singer who has experienced first hand what you have written, I suggest that everyone looking to have a career get this book now!" **David Lee Brewer, Manager, Brewer International, Tenor: Teatro Real, Opera Monte Carlo, Oper Leipzig, German National Theater Weimar, Houston Grand Opera**

"Your ideas sure struck home with me! My career had flourished in Europe but I hadn't worked in the States for over 10 years. I had sworn off auditioning as useless and bad for my mental health! But I was missing the point. I realized I would never sing at the Met or anyplace in the USA without auditioning." **Gregory Reinhart, Bass: MET, New York City Opera, San Francisco Opera, Paris Opera, La Fenice, Aix-en-Provence Festival**

"*Nail Your Next Audition* is fantastic! Warm-hearted and full of humor, it covers the gamut of the audition experience. The exercises are fun to work through." **Margitta Rosales, Soprano: Teatro Verdi Padova, Teatro Guimera di Santa Cruz, Prinz Regent Theater**

"Although I don't have 30 days before I have to sing my first professional role, I have learned so much from your book that I am going there inspired as a result!" **Johanni van Oostrum, Mezzo-Soprano**

Nail Your Next Audition

The Ultimate 30 – Day Guide for Singers

By Janet Williams

Lightning Source 2007

Library of Congress Cataloging-in-Publication Data
Williams, Janet
Nail Your Next Audition, The Ultimate 30 - Day Guide for Singers / Janet Williams
p. cm. Includes bibliographical references and index
ISBN 0-9787521-0-4
1. Singing – Auditions, Psychological Aspects. 2. Acting in Opera. 3. Performance Anxiety. 4. Self Help techniques

Nail Your Next Audition
The Ultimate 30-Day Guide For Singers

Table of Contents

Foreword

Every aspiring professional singer's ultimate desire
is to strut their stuff onstage. All the training and
preparation that we go through is for that single
purpose. We want the opportunity to express the
gift within us in front of an audience that wants to
hear us. Unfortunately many singers have difficulty
getting through the one step that will lead to the
bright lights of the stage: the audition. It is actually
a paradox in itself that singers find the very act of
doing what they love to do, performing in front of
others, so fundamentally different in the audition
setting. It would be so much easier if we could see
the audition itself as a performance and nothing
more than another moment to express our gifts. But
the reality of the audition environment is fraught
with many other factors that often disturb the
"flow" that a singer needs to perform well. Most of
these factors are psychological and can occur when
a singer feels under stress to perform at his/her
absolute best, or in other words, when the stakes are
high.

My own experience with this phenomenon
happened much later in my career, long after my
auditioning days, but in fundamental ways it
mirrored the experiences of participants in my
performance enhancement workshops.

After a near picture perfect run in attaining my
ultimate goal of singing with the world's number
one opera houses, conductors and orchestras; I was
faced with debilitating performance anxiety. It
crept up on me so suddenly that I hardly knew what
had hit me. At the time, I was at the top of the

world - singing at prestigious opera houses and concert halls in the United States, the United Kingdom, Germany, France, Italy, Spain, the Netherlands, Belgium, Israel, Japan and recording with some of the most wonderful musicians in the world, garnering rave reviews and promises of bigger and better things to come. All of my dreams were coming true, until the unthinkable happened. I began to unravel.

At first I thought the quiver that appeared in my voice was a purely technical problem. I searched high and low for answers to the signs, which were a lot like the robot of "Lost in Space" fame crying "Warning! Warning!" Curiously, at first, these signs would all but disappear in my practice sessions with my voice teacher or coaches, but would raise their ugly heads and make their presence known at the most inopportune times: during all-important auditions, or worse yet, onstage in front of thousands of listeners, many of whom were opera aficionados. I was gripped with fear and could no longer concentrate on the music I so loved communicating.

I regrouped and began my search for answers to help with the anxiety that was crippling my vocal abilities and eventually found a lifeline in the teachings of vocal pedagogue David Jones, as well as Alma Thomas, Don Green and Barry Green, each of whom had begun their careers as performance psychologists for top seeded athletes.

Many of the concepts taught by these optimal performance trainers weren't new or foreign to me. I'd been introduced to the importance of positive thinking and self-talk early in my training through my voice teacher and mentor at Indiana University, Professor Camilla Williams. Camilla often noted that, though I was one of the most gifted of her students, I wasn't the most confident one. She'd sprinkle her favorite motivational quotes throughout my lessons, trying to build my confidence and help keep me focused. "Change your thoughts and change your world" was her favorite! "You have to *see* yourself on the stage, singing beautifully. You have to *hear* the applause and anticipate the positive reviews!" Little did I know these same principles would later offer me a lifeline during the crisis in my performing career.

The collective approach to eliciting optimal performance is grounded in mental conditioning, or the building of mental muscle as I came to call it. I believe that mental conditioning provides the foundation to being able to perform optimally under any and all types of stressful circumstances. Certainly the audition environment fits this description.

In *Nail Your Next Audition, The Ultimate 30-Day Guide For Singers*, you will find the teachings of master performance psychologists adapted to the unique needs of singers and pared down to the bare basics that have been tried, tested and proven effective by myself and the many students from my private voice studio, seminars, workshops and master classes. *In each and every case, singers using these techniques have improved their auditioning and performance skills remarkably.* The proof has been seen "in the pudding". They have won contracts and performing opportunities

consistently after incorporating the concepts and
exercises into their daily practice routines.

The 30-day guide will give you concepts and
exercises to incorporate into a systematic daily
practice routine that includes the technical and
interpretive elements singers normally concentrate
on when preparing music for performance – in
addition to the mental training often neglected.

It is my hope that *Nail Your Next Audition, The
Ultimate 30-Day Guide For Singers* will be your
blueprint to achieving optimum performance not
only for auditions, but also throughout your singing
life. Take these lessons that I've learned and the
notes I've been given. Use them to soar to your
highest heights!

Acknowledgments

There are many people in my life who have been inspirational in the writing of this book. Many thanks to celebrated soprano, Professor Camilla Williams for teaching, mentoring, nurturing, motivating and believing in me throughout my singing career. Many thanks as well to vocal pedagogue and master voice teacher David Jones for guiding me through vocal challenges, and encouraging me to teach and to write while giving me the tools to do both effectively. Thanks to my special mentors and colleagues who read the manuscript and gave important suggestions and advice for the finished book. Thanks to my editor, Elaine Bernstein for her eye for detail and gift for organization. Special thanks to my ghost editors Alicia Nails for her special way with words and Brenda Williams for seeing what no other eyes could see. Thanks to my students who continue to inspire me with their dedication, enthusiasm and courage. Thanks to the long list of coaches, directors and conductors with whom I've worked over the years who have contributed much to my development and success as a performer and teacher. A special word of thanks to the pioneering work of performance psychologists and high performance coaches like Barry Green, W. Timothy Gallwey, Professor Don Greene and Dr. Alma Thomas. Finally, thank you to my husband, family and friends, without whose support I could never have pursued my dreams.

INTRODUCTION

Tales From the Trenches

If you find that you're auditioning, but not winning roles, or that you're not consistently performing at your personal best in audition or competition situations, you may just need the proper tools to develop auditioning skills.

Don't worry! Help is here now. You're not alone in your dilemma. In fact, one of the most sought after sopranos in the world today confides that she experienced a period in the early days of her career when she couldn't get hired to save her life! Renée Fleming writes about it candidly in her autobiography, *The Inner Voice, The Making of a Singer*, 2004.

> *"For all the progress I had made with my voice and with languages, style, and musicianship over the years, I had advanced very little in my auditioning skills. I was fine on the stage once the part was mine and I could concentrate on working out its nuances, but in auditions I inevitably felt insecure."* Renée Fleming *(p. 75, The Inner Voice)*

Who would have imagined that this accomplished soprano and international superstar had to overcome huge hurdles to achieve the worldwide acclaim she now enjoys. And she is not unique.

By now, you've heard many tell their own audition or performance meltdown horror stories. Maybe you've even experienced a few of your own and have lived to talk about it. There are myriad reasons why an audition can go really wrong. Here are just a few:

The "Doom Room" – Audition spaces with low ceilings, thick carpet, curtains, or upholstery, small and void of reverb, that swallow up so much of your sound that you feel as if you're singing into a pillow.

The "Waiting Game" – The big cool down after you've warmed up and waited an hour past your allotted audition time.

"Of Human Bondage" – You've been waiting so long that you're beginning to feel more like a hostage than a singer who is no longer warmed up, dying of hunger or thirst with not a practice room, water fountain or snack in sight.

"Grand Central Station" – Your fellow colleagues are coming and going, talking your ear off, and you can no longer concentrate.

"Psst...Over Here" – The auditors are seemingly so engrossed in conversation (or their sandwiches!) they couldn't possibly be listening to you. Or maybe they're discussing that high B-flat that just got away from you?

My personal favorite happened when I auditioned for Claudio Abbado, then music director of the Berlin Philharmonic. I arrived a full half hour before my scheduled singing time, but was immediately pushed onto the stage of the Berlin

Philharmonic Hall still wearing my coat, gloves and ear muffs because the singer scheduled before me hadn't shown up. No waiting game, cool down or other such situation, but these were still somehow not exactly the ideal circumstances for singing such an important audition!

You know what I'm talking about and you know why I call it the "trenches". You're out there fighting for your performing life, improvising under volatile conditions over which you often have no control.

Or do you?

Battle Plans

Did you know that the most important element in any battle is the PLAN?

You might be thinking: "Of course! Everyone knows that you have to plan." But I've been amazed to discover the big difference between the *planning techniques* used by successful auditioners, as compared to those that the less successful ones use.

> Maria Callas gave an acclaimed series of master classes at The Julliard School in 1971. She is quoted as saying: *"There are only three things one needs to make a career as a singer: concentration, technique and courage."*

In my experience, she was right on the money. But what does it take to be able to call on these things at

will, at the exact moment that you need them most?
Again, the answer is - a plan.   You need to have
devised and internalized an effective plan of action.

What you are now reading is a step-by-step, day
–by- day blueprint to developing and incorporating
into your practice, all of the elements needed for
successful auditioning. Actually, these elements
must be present for successful performance of any
kind.

Imagine the excitement of building a plan of action
that will take you from where you are right now,
and help you to develop into a more seasoned,
powerful performer in as little as 30 days!

With *Nail Your Next Audition*, you will do just that!

Give Auditors What They Want – L–O–V–E!

"An audition is really a performance." (*Complete
Preparation, A Guide to Auditioning for Opera,*
Joan Dornemann 1992)

Audition success lies in delivering just what the
auditors are looking and listening for. But just what
do they want? The simple answer may surprise
you.   They want the exact same thing that the
paying audience member wants.

The auditor wants to enjoy your performance!

The good news is, it doesn't take *perfection* to
produce an enjoyable performance. It takes
Likeability + Originality + Vocal Versatility +
Evenness in your delivery.

In short, all you need is **L-O-V-E**.

- Likeability – It is your ability to project a sense of honesty and enjoyment as you communicate to your audience. It is the sharing of your inner commitment, your personal engagement to the music you are singing. *It is the contagious feeling of being one with the music and the moment, with which you "infect" your audience.* It is your ability to project a sense of what the music means to you, as well as who *you* are to those listening.

- Originality - It is that special, not easily definable "something" that no one else but you can bring to the music you are performing. It is your *individual rendition* of the music you perform: your ability to create a performance environment through your vocal color, your physical poise, your focus, and your commitment.

- Vocal Versatility - It is *your individual vocal quality* as a singer: the quality that makes your sound unique, that captures the essence and range of emotions of the character you are portraying or the music you are interpreting and stirs the emotions of the listener.

- Evenness - It is your *reliability* as a singer: the technical and musical precision with which you express your gift *consistently*.

All of the above creates an emotional connection –
an intimate musical relationship between you and
your audience. I call it the love factor.

All you need is L-O-V-E! And here's how you can
get it…

Plan Your T-I-M-E to Nail Your Audition

The successful auditioner has a multi-pronged,
foolproof plan that makes it possible to deliver the
goods for an enjoyable performance – every time.
This plan should be written down and practiced
consistently and in detail, so that the unconscious
mind will automatically revert to its techniques
when you are in performance mode. A successful
plan will include the four essential elements of
optimal performance:

Technical Precision
Inner Awareness
Mental Muscle
Expressive Freedom

In Short, **T-I-M-E.**

Let's examine the four pronged plan to make this
your T-I-M-E at the end of the 30 day countdown:

1. *Technical Precision* –You will learn to
   identify all of the musical and textual cues
   given by the composer and librettist.
   Understanding these cues and what is
   required of you to respond to each one of
   them brings the piece of music to life for
   you. This will allow you to concentrate and

properly interpret the piece throughout your performance.

2. *Inner Awareness* – You will be able to go within and and prepare to sing from your Center. You'll learn to observe what you're feeling and thinking while you sing. This will allow you to uncover and tap into the desire to do what you do at the deepest level of your being- express yourself through song, and to recognize any obstacles in your path. By building a strong connection with your inner awarness, you connect to your inner will or the Self that knows what you're made of at your core. This is the Self that will help you to realize all that you dream of or imagine for your singing life. You will identify your true emotional outlook and confront your – often unconscious– inner obstacles to success. Once faced and transformed to serve your purpose, this Inner Awareness will lead you to fulfill your goals. Aligning your inner awareness with your goals will strengthen your resilience as well.

3. *Mental Muscle* – You will learn to exercise the positive mental attitude that is required to succeed. This means you will set your intention and send yourself positive messages and images as you stretch to attain that goal. This process of disciplining your thought ultimately works to accentuate your strengths and minimize or even eliminate your weaknesses. It helps you to experiment with your senses and train your focus,

attention, awareness and concentration. Exercising your mental muscle consciously gives your subconscious a plan of action to rely upon when unexpected distractions threaten your performance. You'll never be caught off guard again without knowing how to regroup.

4. *Expressive Freedom* – You will master the tools that help you to use your body awareness, physical expression and poise to attain physical freedom of expression for the character you are portraying. This includes identifying and using facial expressions, body stance, physical gestures and shifts of focus that project the emotional meaning and overall environment underlying the text and music you are performing. Expressive freedom is often characterized as poise or a certain ease with which you present yourself while performing. Attaining expressive freedom in performance involves mastering the techniques to become aware of and to release unwanted body tension as well as learning your individual needs for proper physical conditioning. This includes sufficient rest, healthy diet, planning to deal with allergies, acid reflux, colds, menstrual cycles, etc.

In my experience and opinion, the majority of singers who find themselves unsuccessful in auditioning are often incorporating only one or two of these four essential elements in their practice – usually the technical and/or the expressive element. These (often good) singers remain disappointed in the results of their audition efforts until they change their preparation plan.

The reason is: *Optimum performance only occurs when all four of the essential elements are present.* All four elements must be a consistent part of your preparation period in order for you to achieve audition success.

Using this guide, you will decide, detail and nail down every step in your T-I-M-E Plan.

Step Into Your Spotlight

What exactly do you want? It may be a specific role or part, contract, agent or prize. It could be entrance into a prestigious apprentice program or ensemble. Or it could be as general as longevity and success in your singing career. Perhaps it's as simple as a making a steady income as a singer. Stepping into the spotlight of your realized dreams requires that you first define the absolute essence of what it is you want. Only then can you begin a process of working backwards from that ultimate goal or desire and uncovering the path that will lead you into your spotlight – the fulfillment of your intention.

How do you know what you really want?

The amazing thing is that many of us never really fully contemplate this basic, yet essential question.

Identify Your Inner Center Stage Experience

Seek a quiet place and take a moment to go within.
Ask yourself what would make you truly happy?
Can you envision what your life would be like?
How would a typical day in your ideal life be?
What would you like to be able to say you know in
or about your life? How would you like to be with
other people in your life – family, friends, business
colleagues, etc.? What would you like to learn and
grow from during your lifetime? What would you
like to be able to say you mastered or accomplished
in your life? What would you like to learn about
yourself in this life? Be honest with yourself and the
answers will reveal your true desires. Your true
desires will help you formulate what you intend to
do in your life. Your intentions will direct your
actions and your actions will lead you into the
spotlight of your accomplished goal.

Now write it all down.

(See Intention Revelation Worksheet, p. 89)

Using what you learned in the Intention Revelation
exercise, you'll discover and record your intentions
for your future. Look at what your quiet moments
revealed. Based upon what you wrote, what do you
really want? Why? What will be the desired
outcome of having what you want? Will you be
happy, rich, healthy, fulfilled or successful? This
answer will further reveal your inner will or desire.
Now write your answers as if what you desire has
already materialized. What will your life be like?
How will you interact in your world? How will you
feel emotionally? Your desire will speak to you

from the depths of your being and this "powerful voice" that speaks to your innermost Self will be the guiding force in helping you attain what you say you really want. This power inside of you knows *how* to make it happen!

(See Intended Accomplishment Worksheets, pp. 91-92)

Clear the Path to Your Inner Center Stage

"Whatever man feels deeply or images clearly, is impressed upon the subconscious mind, and carried out in minutest detail." (The Game Of Life and How to Play It, Florence Shovel Shinn, 1905)

Do you ever find yourself saying that you want to win a certain competition or role, but secretly or subconsciously telling yourself all the reasons it could never happen: "I'll never get it, so why bother." "I'm sure they've already cast the part." "I'm not good enough yet," or "I'm not half as good as so and so, so I probably won't get it." "Oh well, if I don't get it, it wasn't meant to be." All of this negative thinking and sabotaging self-talk *before* you even sing a note! These are concrete examples of not being clear within.

Often, once you know what you want, doubts and obstacles appear that slow or prevent you from reaching your goal. When this happens, there is usually some internal conflict about what you say you want and how you currently *think* and *act* in relation to you getting what you desire. The doubting self-talk reveals the areas where you're not clear within yourself. This conflict must be recognized and resolved before you can move closer to your spotlight.

If you're not clear, if you can't clearly imagine getting what you want – you can't even allow yourself to *hope* for the best. Your task in such instances is to align your thoughts, words and actions with your intent to reach your ultimate goal: getting what you want! By resolving inner conflict, you will experience harmony between your inner desires and your outer actions. When your thoughts, words and actions are aligned with your ultimate desire, you have made a huge step toward getting what you want and stepping into your spotlight.

Melanie* is a singer without the ability to recognize or say what is good about her performance abilities. She simply can't recognize and acknowledge the things she does well. Whenever she sings a phrase, she waits for someone to criticize it, and when no criticism comes, she criticizes herself. But to be a successful performer, it is just as important to know what you do well as it is to know where you need improvement. Melanie's mental blockage to her success is her own negative self-talk, which cannot possibly support her goals to perform well. In fact, Melanie is sabotaging her intention and undermining her own attempts to fulfill her goals. Any kind of consistent self-talk is an unerring self-fulfilling prophecy, whether it is positive or negative.

*All names have been changed for reasons of privacy.

Clearing the path to your inner center stage requires that you uncover the fears that keep you from claiming and having what you want. Only by uncovering your fear can you stop sabotaging your intention to step into the spotlight. What is the negative self-talk actually protecting you from? Why are you afraid of claiming what you say you want? Uncover your fears. Are you afraid you won't live up to other people's expectations? Are you afraid you might fail? Are you afraid you just might succeed? What would failure or success mean to you and your life? Are you afraid that your success might change the way you interact with your family or close friends? Are you afraid you won't be liked or you'll have to make changes that are uncomfortable for you?

Only *you* can answer the questions. Only *you* can free yourself from any fear that blocks the path to your success. Don't be afraid to face them head on and clear them from your thoughts, words and actions. Write your thoughts as they come to you.

(See Clear From Fear Worksheets, pp. 93-98)

Cindy*, an exceptionally gifted soprano who has performed for two consecutive summers with a well-known apprentice program, was a participant in my seminar "The Art of Auditioning". I was blown away by the sheer beauty and power of her voice, yet she had been auditioning for more than a year without signing with an agent or landing a contract.
I quickly realized that a very important performance element was missing. When Cindy sang, there was nothing in her physical presence that made you

believe the plight of her character. She sang well, but it was just a beautiful sound without much emotional connection to her persona in the form of physical expressions in the face and body.

Since there are techniques that address this performance component, I asked myself how this major element could go undetected by Cindy for so long. After some "one-on-one" work, the answer revealed itself. Cindy had never actively sought the answer to the question: "Why am I not getting any further toward reaching my goal?" Instead, she had convinced herself that all control was out of her hands. The results were somehow "meant (or not meant) to be".

I asked her about the most basic step required for success – her audition routine – I was shocked to learn that she had no structured routine. This gifted singer simply showed up and hoped for the best. She had no plans for directing her thoughts or creating a performance environment. There was no specific plan for refocusing in case of distractions or nervous energy. There was no process to access the depth and specific meaning in the text she was communicating. Her thoughts were free to roam wherever they wanted. Hence the disconnected and uninvolved performance she projected.

Cindy's biggest mistake in the whole process was to cede responsibility for her progress to fate, rather than trying to find the answers to clear obvious blocks in the path to her success. Once she reclaimed personal responsibility for lack of progress toward her goals, she empowered herself to make the necessary adjustments in order to move forward.

Clear yourself of all internal blocks to your intention, whether they are in your thoughts, your self-talk, your words or your actions. Face and release your fears. It is the key to clearing the path to your inner center stage and stepping into your spotlight!

Me! Me! -Me! Me! - Me! Me! Me!

Now that you know what you want and have gotten clear about it, answer these last questions. Are you willing to focus all of your power and energy on your success? Are you willing to put yourself first? Are you willing to garner all of your resources in order to achieve your aim?

Are you willing to act on these notes?

- Are your technical skills up to snuff for your chosen audition repertoire? If not, are you willing to identify the vocal exercises and body awareness that will help you to gain the needed skills and perform them consistently?

- If you find it unrealistic that you will be able to execute the necessary skills consistently at the end of the 30-day countdown, are you willing to choose an aria more suitable to your present ability?

- Are you lacking dramatic skills that are needed to create a character? Are you willing to take steps to seek out the help you need? If you want to sing in a staged production, but you only have concert experience, are you willing to take a few acting or movement classes or seek private coaching from an actor or drama coach before your audition? Such steps ensure that you're taking the small steps that are necessary to achieve your ultimate goal. These are the process goals that Dan Green describes in his book, *Performance Success,* 2002.

- Is your mental muscle in need of training? Do you find your thoughts working for you or against you? What are you willing to do to make sure that you're thinking appropriate, helpful thoughts in line with your intention, before you audition? Are you willing to do what it takes to sharpen your concentration and focusing skills?

- Are you listening to the people you trust? Are you willing to listen and do what is suggested?

- If you don't agree, or if you find you aren't progressing at a reasonable rate toward your goals with your present coach or teacher, are you willing to listen to your inner guide and follow your instincts even if it means risking a friendship or relationship?

Think about this long and hard. If you are willing, you'll have to make a commitment to yourself to follow through with the work that will get you to where you want to be. The process of commitment provides the inspiration to constructing your plan of action – your next step.

Plan The Steps To Your Spotlight

Once your thoughts, words and actions are aligned with your intention, your path is clear to your inner center stage, and you are willing to do what it takes to reach your goal, you must then plan the necessary steps to get you to your spotlight.

Carl* is a student at a major German "Hochschule" who had been assigned a voice teacher with whom he could not connect. His voice, a natural lovely lyric baritone, was always reliable. After several months working with the teacher, Carl found himself struggling to reach notes that used to come easily to him. Because the music department required that he study with this teacher, his only obvious choices were to either give up or continue to suffer vocal decline.

But Carl saw beyond those limited choices. Instead, he decided to look outside of his university for help. He found a voice teacher who was willing to work with him under his difficult circumstances. His voice not only responded, but also flourished and grew. Carl did not accept his "fate". He recognized the problem, took action and found a solution to his dilemma.

He continued to pursue his studies and was rewarded with a healthy vocal technique that could serve him during a difficult period. He trusted his inner voice and instinct and he followed through by seeking to find what he needed.

It is during this phase that you create your Plan of Action. These are the building block steps between where you are now and where you need to be in order for your intention to be realized. Your ability to remain focused on these areas until you see the results of progress will be the final step in attaining your goal.

Keeping Your Eye on the Prize

Staying focused on what you want and being willing to work to get it will result in your remaining in the present moment, which is where magic happens! Remaining in the present means releasing the past and letting the future evolve, as it must. This is the main reason for writing out a plan of action.

A plan of action demands that you focus on what your intention is – what you want rather than what happened the last time or what might happen in the future. It also gives you the blueprint you need to stay on course and see every result as opportunity for further movement toward your intention. When you're focused, it's easier to let go of the need to influence the outcome. You're too involved in doing what you need to do to get the results you want.

Remember the five steps to reaching the spotlight of your success. They are the foundation for your battle plan.

1. Identify your unique "Center Stage" experience and intend to have it.

2. Clear the path to your inner center stage.

3. Be willing to do what needs to be done in order to get to the spotlight.

4. Plan the path leading to the spotlight of your accomplished intention.

Stay focused on the spotlight until you are standing in it.

Get Ready, Get Set...

Before you begin your personal 30-day countdown to nailing your next audition, I want you to think about a very important element of your success in implementing your Plan, your support network.

Who Can You Count On?

> Think of four to five people on whom you can depend for support in reaching your singing goals. These are the people who know you and believe in you, who tell you the truth, who encourage and inspire you. The people in your support network will be active participants in your plan of action. This list of people should include a musician, coach or voice teacher, and your pianist, as well as anyone else who knows

your voice and whom you trust to give you
honest and constructive criticism and advice.

➤ Once you identify them, ask each of them to
commit to attending at least one of the three
mock auditions during the next four weeks
to listen and comment upon your progress.
Be sure to plan a mutually agreeable time,
date and place for these performances with
your pianist and support network.

➤ Share your plan of action with each person
in your support network so that they know
what your goals are. Sharing your intention
also gives witness of it outside of yourself –
an effective motivating factor toward
accomplishing your goals.

The next important step is an exercise in self-
awareness. It will involve the opinions of your
mentor, voice teacher or coach about your aria
selections and suitability as well as the types
auditions you should seek to sing at this stage of
your development.

Who Do You Want To Hear You Now?

One of the most important decisions you will make
is which audition you should go for. There are
many types of auditions. In your early training you
may have to audition for admittance to a voice
program, or for a particular voice teacher or coach.
In many competitions, there is an initial audition in
the form of a recording that must be submitted
before you can even compete. There are auditions

for university or community opera scenes or productions as well as for solo parts in oratorios.

At the next stage of your training, auditions for apprentice programs, national and international competitions, agents, conductors and opera companies become necessary.

At every stage or your development, there are auditions that could be viewed as "practice auditions", where your view of the audition is merely that of an opportunity to practice and improve your audition skills. For such occasions, it would be wise to choose auditions that are not highly visible, high stakes occasions. Auditions for parts in university opera productions and choral works, local or university competitions, summer stock musicals, or small summer festivals can all be viewed as "practice" auditions.

The most important consideration is choosing such practice opportunities carefully. Practice auditions should be those where your expectations are not high and you don't have a lot to lose in participating. These are as a rule, not career building steps.

Save your "big auditions" for the moments you want to use as stepping-stones to your spotlight. These are the auditions that matter most to the fulfillment of your ultimate dreams. Auditions that fall into this category are strategic career building possibilities. For such auditions, it is generally prudent to have had some audition "practice" before participating. These auditions include:

- The national or international competition, where you're vying with many other singers for a monetary prize;

- The major national opera apprentice programs;

- The international summer opera apprentice programs;

- The "Introductory Platform", where you sing for someone (potential sponsor, conductor, director, general manager, agent or mentor, etc.) whom you hope will consider using or supporting you in the future or over a period of time. In this instance, the audition is not only about a particular role or contract, but your overall potential development as an artist. In such an audition you would want to show the full range of your talent as well as your *growth potential.*

These auditions are some of the most important building blocks in a young singer's career. Such auditions are not advised for the beginner and should be undertaken only after the singer has had some performance experience of a professional nature and lots of previous audition practice.

You, the singer, empower yourself when you choose your auditions well.

The Right Choice

When I gave a seminar on "The Art of Auditioning", the most shocking discovery occurred when I asked the participants to describe why they chose to sing the arias on their lists.

More specifically, I asked, "What makes your rendition of this aria so special?" I got all manner of vague answers: "I really relate to the text and express it well." "My diction is stellar." "I feel like I relate well to the character." " I love the music."

Every possible combination of answers except the most important one: "I sing this aria fabulously!" "I love my sound in this aria." "This aria shows off my wonderful floating B- flat or my impressive coloratura or my exciting high C!"

Totally missing was the excitement that singers usually associate with what *they* bring to the aria. I took it a step further. "What do you most like about your vocal quality? How would you describe your biggest vocal advantage? What is the quality in your voice that makes people not only want to hear it but to *pay* to hear it as well, and to hear *you* singing this aria? What makes your voice and presence as an artist singing this aria, stand out among the crowd?"

No one, *not one person* could answer these questions! My reply: "If you don't know what it is, how will anyone else? If you don't love, respect, honor your sound, then who else will? Why should they?"

What do you have to offer that is unique? What are the vocal qualities that make your sound stand out? Do you know them? Can you name them? How do you sell or accentuate your positives and improve or neutralize your weaker points?

Here I must quote my wonderful colleague, the veteran character tenor Steven Cole:

" Technique is all about maximizing what you can do and minimizing what you can't."

If you had to describe your personal "LOVE" factors as a singer and as a performer, what would they be? Which arias in your repertoire show these factors to their fullest potential.

"Your audition list works best if it informs your listeners instead of confusing them." (Joan Dornemann, *Complete Preparation, A Guide to Auditioning for Opera,* 1992)

Famed Coach, Joan Dornemann advocates audition repertoire that best shows what you do well now, and includes one aria that shows what your voice will likely be able to do in the future. With that in mind, answer these questions:

1. Are the arias you have chosen representative of the best work you do now; are they within your grasp technically now?

2. Would you be suitable technically and physically to sing the entire role from

which the aria is taken, now or in the near future?

3. Is the aria under five minutes long?

4. Is the aria translated and memorized?

5. Do the selections on your list include a variety of languages, styles, tempi and emotional landscapes? Remember, you want to show the broad spectrum of your talent.

6. Most importantly, can you imagine singing these arias *well* under the most extreme stress imaginable – during competitive performing, in the 30-day time span you have allotted?

If you and your network of musical supporters cannot answer **yes** to all of these questions, you need to consider another aria selection for this 30-day countdown period. For the best outcome, only include arias for which you can answer **yes** to all of the above questions.

...GO!

THE ULTIMATE 30-DAY GUIDE

The Countdown:
You will need an accompanist on Days 30, 23, 22, 16, 15, 10, 8 and 4

Day 30

Confirm the date, time and place of your first mock audition with your accompanist and support network.

Begin Day 30 by "centering" yourself. There are many methods for centering and relaxation. The most important elements in the centering process are being in a quiet personal space, deep rhythmic breathing and clearing the mind so that you can direct your focus where you want it. The reason it is so important to center yourself before you sing, or do anything goal-oriented, is that only then can you clearly form your intended outcome.

Remember, the first step to success is to identify your inner center stage experience and intend to have it. What I assume you want is to nail your auditions at the end of this 30-day countdown. It is up to you to clear the path to your inner center stage, your innermost desire. You must commit to identifying any obstacles and working to release them during the next 30 days. Centering will help you clearly see what you need to concentrate on during your daily practice sessions. These will be the steps to your spotlight.

Of the many methods for accessing your center I prefer that of Sports Psychologist Don Greene,

PhD. In his book, *Performance Success,* 2002, Dr. Greene describes a step-by-step process of learning to access your Center quickly.

Accessing Your Inner Center Stage

- Sit in a comfortable position with your hands in your lap.

- Formulate in your mind, your intended accomplishment at the end of the 30-day countdown.

- Now, choose a point at a good distance in front of you, below eye level to direct all of your energy. Perhaps it is back wall of the room or hall you are in, a chair or row of seats, a music stand or any object that is below your eye level. This stimulates right brain activity, which helps raise optimum performance levels. Narrow your focus on the object or spot until it moves out of focus. The effect is similar to starring off into space or daydreaming. If this is difficult at first, close your eyes and continue breathing deeply for a few breath cycles and relax into your Center.

- Now, focus your attention on your breathing from a point deep within the center of your being. Imagine a point in your center, just below your navel and two inches inside your body. Inhale through your nose into this point. Fill your torso and rib cage with air. Slowly exhale through your mouth at a steady count until all the air is released. As the air is exhaled, notice any tension you feel in your body and release it, slowly moving from your head to your feet. Concentrating only on your breathing will also quiet any busy chatter in your mind. Repeat this until you feel completely relaxed and focused on your breathing at the center of your body. Enjoy the grounded and calm feeling at your Center.

• When you have been breathing in your Center for several breath cycles, formulate your intention for the end of the 30-day countdown in your mind. (Ex. At the end of the 30-day countdown, I intend to be able to sing my auditions as I would a performance." Take the time to imagine yourself executing what you intend to accomplish. What would help you to do that? Formulate trigger words or phrases that will help you accomplish your goal. (Ex. "Easy flow", "Relaxed Concentration, "Have fun") Repeat these trigger words or phrases as you breath in and out until you can see yourself singing before an audition panel with an easy flow; relaxed but concentrated and having fun. Imagine how good it will feel and how happy it will make you. Speak your intention out loud.

• Now, imagine your energy, your power source gathering at your Center and spinning up through your body out to your point of focus as you open your eyes. Sense the direct connection between your Center and

the source of energy or power you are now
focusing on. This energy will help you
accomplish your intended goal.
Acknowledge it as your partner and decide
to "nail it!"

Refer to your **Intention Revelation Worksheet** on
page 85. Now get specific and write what this 30-
day guide will mean for your performing life. What
will nailing your audition mean for your life?

(See My 30-Day Intention Statement, p. 99)

Your Best L-O-V-E Performance Experience

By now, you've had at least one performance or
moment in a performance when everything worked.
You sang well, you felt confident and sure, you
nailed a difficult note or phrase, you were "in the
flow", you had fun and all was well with the world.
During this performance, your audience
experienced the ultimate synchronicity of
Likeability-Originality-Vocal Versatility-Evenness
that you projected. You most likely felt elated,
happy, excited and you radiated that positive energy
to your audience. The resulting performance
moment was like magic.

Now recall that moment when you felt at one with
your voice, the music, your fellow musicians and
your audience and describe it in minute detail.

**(See Personal Best Assessment Worksheets, pp.
100-101)**

What does L-O-V-E in perfect sync feel like? Ask
yourself the following questions and add any
additional memories that come to mind.

*What did it feel like to be in the flow of the
performance?*
*What sensation or emotions did you feel when you
performed well?*
How did your body feel while you were singing?
Before singing? After singing?
Describe your voice, the sound, texture, and timbre.
*Describe how it felt while singing and how it
sounded to your ear.*
How did the space around you feel?
*What pictures or words come close to describing
the experience, the way you sang, your relationship
to those on stage with you, etc.?*

If you can remember, write down all you did to
prepare, as well as your routine during the days
before and the day of your performance. What did
you eat? How much sleep/rest did you get? What
was your state of mind before the performance?
Where was your energy/stimulation level on a scale
of 1 to 10 with 1 being "sluggish" and 10 being
"manic"?

What I *Can* Do

The next exercise will utilize the results of the Personal Best Assessment worksheet to form a list of positive statements about your abilities as a performer, or what I call *Performance Affirmations*.

(See Performance Affirmations Worksheet, p. 102)
Looking over your Personal Best Assessment, circle or underline all positive adjectives or adverbs you wrote down. For instance, let's say your assessment contains the following sentence or something similar. The underlined words are the ones you would write down at the top of your Performance Affirmations Worksheet and would be used to write positive statements of fact, in the present tense, about the way you perform.

" While singing, my voice <u>filled the hall</u>, the <u>high notes</u> were <u>easy</u> and <u>warm</u>, my body felt <u>relaxed</u> and I sang with a <u>variety</u> of colors and dynamics. I felt as if the music just <u>flowed</u> out of me <u>effortlessly</u>."

Using the underlined words, form sentences *in the present tense* describing your abilities as a performer. These are statements or truth based on reality. You experienced them personally at least once. There is no reason why these experiences cannot repeat themselves again. These are *absolute truths* about your ability as a performer. Now, form your performance affirmations based upon the underlined verbs and adjectives.

My voice fills the hall.
My high notes are warm and easy.
My body is relaxed while performing.
My voice has a variety of colors and dynamics.
The music flows out of me effortlessly.

Practice Session

You will need your accompanist for this session.

Ideal, Quick and Worst Case Scenario Warm-Up Exercises

1. Identify and write down a set of warm-up exercises for the following three scenarios:

    • **Ideal** (for use under perfect conditions, no time constraints, physically healthy)

    • **Quick** (for use when your voice is awake, responsive and fresh, "well-oiled", or exercises that help your voice to warm up quickly)

    • **Worst Case** (for use when you're tired or under the weather, after waiting a long time before you're called to sing, or for particular technical difficulties like releasing tongue tension or unlocking blocked airflow.)

(See Warm-Up Exercises Worksheet, p. 103)

Don't be tempted to skip this exercise! While it may seem unnecessary, it is a very important step in the process of preparing for all possibilities. With preparation comes a sense of calm in the midst of any gathering storm!

2.   You will begin each practice session with Centering and formulating your intention for the session. In this case, you will use the same process as you did for centering on Day 30. But the intentions will be more specific and correspond to what you intend to accomplish during the day's session. In this case, your intention will be to sing through your arias in performance mode to the best of your present ability. See yourself warming up just for this purpose and imagine yourself singing through your arias. As you picture yourself singing well, identify your own trigger words that would make that happen.

• Begin by sitting comfortably.

• State your intention for the session.

• Find a point of focus in front of you, below eye level and direct all your energy toward that point until the point of focus goes soft. Or close your eyes and concentrate on your breathing rhythm. Inhale through your nose and exhale through your mouth for several cycles.

• Direct your inner focus to your center, just below your navel and

about two inches inside your body.
Continue breathing into your center
and formulate trigger words or
phrases that assist you in
accomplishing your intended goal, in
this case singing your audition arias
in performance mode. (Ex. Easy,
Relax, Ready, Flow, etc.)

• Gather your inner power and energy
and direct it outside of your body to
your point of focus. Feel your
connection to your power source and
acknowledge it as your partner as
you intend to "nail it".

3.   Record your arias with your
accompanist. This initial recording can
be done during a voice lesson or
coaching session, but it is important that
you sing each aria through without
stopping, in *performance mode*. Be sure
that the time between pieces is no more
than a minute or two. *No matter what,
once you begin the aria, sing it through
to the end.* Sing it as you would in an
audition or performance situation.

You may want to start with the aria that
is easiest for you, or with the aria with
which you will begin your audition.

Be aware of the physical sensations and
mental focus you notice while singing,
especially at difficult sections of the aria.

- Is there any unwanted body tension?

- Does your attention wander?

- Are you able to re-focus quickly?

- Do you notice any negative self-talk?

- *Try to be aware without judging what you notice.* Simply make a quick mental note of whatever comes to your mind while you're performing.

4.   Before ending the day's session, and *before listening to the recording*, complete the Initial Recording Oberservations Worksheets.

(See Initial Recording ObservationsWorksheets pp. 104-113)

Make notes about how you felt the performance went, what could have been better, where and when you felt tension in your body, how you maintained focus, etc. Often our impressions while singing don't match what we actually hear on a recording. Therefore it's important to have a comparison of what you felt and what you actually hear once you listen to the recording. You can listen to the recording today if you want, but you will not begin to work with it until tomorrow.

5.   Make sure you label the recording with
       the starting date as well as *Day 30,
       Initial Recording.*

Day 29

Today you will listen to your recording and assess
your arias individually in terms of the essential
T-I-M-E elements of optimal performance:

- **Technical Proficiency**
- **Inner Awareness**
- **Mental Muscle**
- **Expressive Freedom.**

From this assessment, you will make your personal
list of process and end goals for each of your arias.

The Aria Assessment Worksheets will be your
guideline for the next four weeks. In them, you will
identify where you are right now with your arias in
terms of the presence of the essential T-I-M-E
elements of optimum performance, and you will
formulate your action and ultimate goals. These
worksheets will serve as the blueprint for getting
where you want to be at the end of your 30-day
countdown.

In terms of percentage, an aria is generally ready for
performance when you feel it is at the 90 % stage of
readiness. That means that for 90% of the time, you
are able sing with technical proficiency, awareness
of your inner will, mental focus and concentration
on the task at hand, and with freedom in your
physical expression of the emotional environment
of the music and character. If you can perform your

aria consistently at 90 % effectiveness, you're right on track to achieving flow in your performance.

(See Aria Assessment Worksheets, pp. 114-121)

1. Listen to your Initial Recording one aria at a time and this time write down your observations. Compare whether or not your initial impressions from yesterday match what you actually hear on the recording.

2. Rate how successful you were integrating each of the essential T-I-M-E elements in your arias on a scale of 1 to 10, with 10 being "very successful" and 1 being "completely unsuccessful".

   - **Technical Proficiency**: How would you rate your overall vocal timbre and quality, diction, dynamic gradations, phrasing, rhythmic and pitch precision, musical decisions and the skill you use implementing them? How is your diction and how well do you use the language and its expressive qualities to add meaning to your musical and vocal delivery and indicate your intentions about the piece?

   - **Inner Awareness**: Is the joy and commitment you have to singing evident? Is there a sense of inner confidence in your sound? Are you expressing the text or merely singing words? How successful were you in

communicating your rea
singing this aria?

- **Mental Muscle**: The
which you move between
concentrated focus (actively
thinking, planning, executing, left-
brain emphasis) and passive focus
(in the present moment, in the flow,
enjoying singing, feeling, intuition,
effortless, outside of your "thinking"
self, right-brain emphasis) is
determined by the mental cues you
give yourself throughout the piece.
The ability to switch between
concentrated, active focus and
"flow" or being in the present
moment, will either save or destroy
your presentation, especially in the
face of the inevitable unknown or
unexpected factors that can make a
performance go wrong. How
successful were you in dealing with
any distractions like noise, negative
self-talk, mistakes or lapses in
concentration?

- **Expressive Freedom**: This is often
the most difficult element to assess
in the absence of a mirror or video
recorder. Simply listening to a
recording doesn't always give a clear
indication of what was going on with
you physically. For instance, many
singers in my workshops *think* they
are using shifts in eye focus,

appropriate facial expressions, physical gestures, body posture, stance and movement, when in fact, very little of that is actually coming across. For our purposes at this point, assess how successful you were at remaining focused on the words and the emotions of the character, as well as how well you anticipated the change in emotions or focus throughout the aria. You can best assess these qualities by listening for colors, dynamic changes, varying levels of intensity and power in your voice. How well were you able to convey a dramatic understanding of your character and communicate your understanding and feelings about what he or she is experiencing? Can you *hear* the emotional element you wish to communicate?

3. Using the **Aria Assessment Worksheets**, make your 30-day countdown goals for each aria, making sure they are challenging but reachable. What do you want to achieve with each aria at the end of the 30-day countdown? This should be listed as an *end* or *ultimate* goal for each piece. What you have to do to achieve it will result in your *process* or *action* goal.

(See 30-Day Aria Goals Worksheets, pp. 122-140)

What tools or techniques can you use to achieve your goals? If the problem was technical, do you need to isolate that passage and repeat it daily before performing the piece? If it was physical, can you isolate exactly which muscles tense up or the sequence of events leading to the tension or energy problems? If it is mental, what trigger words can help you immediately re-focus? If it is inner awareness, what steps can you make before beginning to set up your intentions for the performance of the piece?

- Write down a tangible goal that would show up after having used specific tools or techniques. For instance, " I will use a specific word at the same specific point in the aria over a one-week period, to trigger the focus I need in order to stay low in my body for the high note." If at the end of that period your mind automatically uses the trigger word and it helps alleviate the problem, your goal has been reached.

- Identify your **trigger** words and phrases that most likely elicit the type of reaction in you that brings about your desired goal for the piece. If you want to sing a phrase without taking a breath, maybe a trigger word/phrase for you would be "low breath" or "flow". If you'd like to sing a high note pianissimo, perhaps a word for you would be "float" or "silvery". Often a dynamic or harmonic progression has a special color. What would that color be?

> Pavarotti is famous for using sensory elements like colors as triggers to describe the way a tone should sound. For him, a high C could be more specific than red or purple– red became crimson or bordeau, purple could be amethyst, violet or lilac, giving the tone much more detail and depth.

Some trigger words are mental or inner feelings: "relax", "easy", "free", "sound washing over", while others are more physical or technical: "tongue forward", "sit", "high palate", "loose jaw" etc.

Trigger words can be adjectives, verbs, adverbs, sensory words having to do with a smell, texture, color, taste, etc. As long as it captures the essence of *what* you'd like to do or communicate, and *how* you'd like to do it, the trigger can be useful.

(See Aria Trigger Words Worksheets, pp. 141-148)

4. The final exercise for today is to create your **Performance Environment** for each aria. This involves analyzing your character's environment at the moment he or she sings the aria.

    It is important to know what has happened to make him or her sing at this moment. What is his or her emotional situation at the moment? What are the physical surroundings like? What time is it? What time of year is it? Is he or she alone? If not, who is there and what is their relationship to your character? What does the music suggest?

Also important is the physical condition of the character. How old is he or she? Is he or she healthy or sick, or somehow incapacitated? What does the music suggest? How can you physically portray the character?

(See Performance Environment/Character Analysis Worksheets, pp. 149-156)

Think again of trigger words or phrases that come to mind when you picture your character physically as he or she sings. Is the character happy or ecstatic? Is he or she frightened or resigned or both? Is he or she physically uncomfortable or excited? Is he or she painfully shy or extroverted? Stoic, dignified? Is he or she hungry or cold? Is he or she privileged or poor? How would you describe the emotions your character expresses? How would you physicalize them? Are you the same sex as the character or the opposite? How does one physicalize the opposite sex? What has happened to your character up to this point in the story?
All those experiences make up who the character is now. All those experiences will add to your performance environment.

Write down four to six trigger words or phrases that come to mind to describe the physical environment, emotional and physical state of the character.

(See Performance Environment Trigger Words Worksheets, pp. 157-158)

Review your list and then circle two or three words from each list that most closely resonate with you.

These are your trigger words for your Performance Environment. Before you begin to sing your arias in performance mode, you will take a moment to recall these words or phrases and trigger all the emotions, physical reactions and body stances, gestures, etc. that these words elicit.

Day 28

Today you will begin what I call "Conscious Practicing". In a conscious practice session, you begin by going within or centering yourself and stating your intention or goals for the session. Then you work with your specific action goals throughout the session. Make sure you record your session.

Center yourself and state your intention for today's practice session. Focus upon the trigger words that you've identified to help you reach your goals for your first aria. Inhale and exhale thinking the trigger words you will employ to help you technically, mentally or physically.

1. Record your session.

2. Select two arias to concentrate on today.

3. Practice incorporating your trigger words or phrases into your singing.

4. Practice only the sections of the aria you are working to improve. Take a few bars before the section begins and practice it until you've begun to feel improvement.

5. Repeat the above for the second aria.

6. Take a short break (five to ten minutes) and go outside of the practice room. (Keep the recorder going) Before re-entering the room, center yourself with the intention to "nail it!" during a run-through of both arias in performance mode. Outside the room, review your trigger words for the goals in your aria and where you want to recall them while singing. Remind yourself of your performance environment trigger words before entering the room.

7. Re-enter the room, create your performance environment and sing the first aria through in performance mode (without interruptions). Take a moment to remind yourself of your trigger words for the second aria goals, create your performance environment and then sing

the second aria through in the same manner.

8. Make notes about what you noticed during the performance. Were you successful in focusing on your performance environment? Were there attention lapses? Where? Were you able to recall the trigger words where planned? Do you need to recall them sooner? Later? Was there any unwanted tension in your body?

9. End the practice session and turn off the recorder.

10. Take a break, then listen to the recording and revise your goals if needed. Prioritize your goals for tomorrow's session. What needs the most work? How much time do you need to give it?

Day 27

Repeat yesterday's session practicing the same arias with any goal revisions you made yesterday. Begin the session with centering and focusing upon the trigger words that helped yesterday. Revise your trigger words if necessary.

Day 26

Today you will work on the remaining two arias in the same manner in which you worked the first two.

Day 25

Repeat yesterday's session with any revisions you made yesterday.

Day 24

Re-confirm with this week's support network listener and your accompanist. You will need to perform in front of them on Day 22.

Shifts of Focus
Today's session will incorporate one final exercise that is vital to the overall presentation of your arias. It identifies the shifts in focus that occur during your aria and anticipates them a beat or two before they happen with shifts in eye focus or simple changes in your physical stance or position of your head.

While this may seem a bit controlled or planned, it is actually something you do daily in your natural conversation style. You think, *and then* you react. As you think, your eyes are sometimes unfocused or focused out in the distance and when you begin to speak, your head changes position, your eyes focus on the person you're speaking to, on a definite object or in a definite direction at specific moments, depending upon the emphasis you want to give what you're saying.

1.   Imagine your aria as a normal
      conversation with someone or with
      yourself. If you were to speak the words
      instead of singing them, where would
      the natural shifts in focus occur? When
      would your body register that shift? In
      normal conversations, first you think it,
      then you prepare it and finally you say it.
      Try doing the same while singing and
      your interpretation takes on much more
      realism and deeper meaning.

2.   Use the music to help you determine
      your shifts. Composers are often very
      good at indicating a shift in focus with
      harmonic or rhythmic changes or short
      musical interludes.

3.   Now, using your own personal
      shorthand, mark the moments in your
      score where the focus shifts for your
      character. Where does he or she begin a
      new thought, take off in another
      direction, or repeat a phrase? In the case
      of lots of repeats, how can you make
      sense of the repetitions? How can you
      prepare those shifts in focus with your
      physical expressions or eye focus?
      These do not have to be big, broad
      movements. In fact, subtle works best!
      A shift or tilt of the head, a slight
      expressive movement of one hand, a
      shift of weight from one leg to another,
      often work wonders to convey that
      something meaningful is about to occur.

The timing and intensity are what matters most in shifts of focus.

4.   Practice focusing and shifts in focus using your trigger words, based on your goals for the piece. Try to maintain your intended focus points until the shift occurs in the music or text.

5.   Make notes about how successful you've been in anticipating and shifting focus during your practice sessions.

Day 23

You will need an accompanist for the second half of this practice session.

During today's session, you will practice only the process goals in each of the four arias for the first half of your session. You will take a break outside of the practice room and return after centering and intending to "nail it" by singing all four arias in performance mode.

Your primary goal should be to incorporate your planned trigger words, focus points and shifts in focus, into each aria.

Make sure your recorder is on.

Day 22: Mock Audition #1

Before the mock audition:

- Today, begin your session as normal with centering and intending to "nail it" during your mock performance.

- Warm up with the appropriate exercises.

- Read over your **performance affirmations** and your aria **trigger words** and **shifts of focus** for the aria you will sing first.

At the mock performance:

- Make sure you have paper and pen for the audience member(s) to make notes and leave written feedback. Let the person or people know what you've concentrated on this week and ask them to observe whether those things are present.

- Make sure the tape recorder is on.

- Before entering the room or stage, recall your trigger words for your performance environment. Center again and intend to "nail it!".

- Enter the room and introduce your piece as you would in an actual audition situation.

- Your audience member(s) will select the next pieces.

- Take enough time between each piece to re-focus and create your new performance environment.

After the mock performance:

(See Mock Audition #1 Observations Worksheets, pp. 159-163)

- Make sure to collect your feedback sheets and thank your audience for being there.

- Make detailed notes after your mock performance as to how you felt before, during and after each aria in terms of the T-I-M-E goals you've been working on all week. Be sure to write what went well as well as what needs more work. Try to write all your observations in a positive vein!

Imagine you are a professional athlete giving an interview after a major tournament or match: whether they win or lose, athletes always find a way to put a positive spin on things. There's always something positive that happened, and even when things didn't go at all well, athletes find a positive way of looking at what needs to be worked on and how to make the next game better.

Technical:

I was able to recall my trigger words and they seemed to make the difficult passages easier to sing. I need to find another trigger word for the high B-flat in …

Inner:

I was psyched and ready to sing well at the beginning. I was able to remind myself what I do well and why I chose to sing this aria. My nerves were still at a high level. I need to work on lowering my adrenaline.

Mental:

I was able to keep my focus and concentration during the first piece, but noticed my attention wandering between pieces to other things like, what is my audience thinking? I have to practice my positive self-talk in order to bring myself back on track in an instant.

Expressive Freedom:

I had more trouble remembering my focus points in the second aria. I didn't feel as if my body language conveyed what I was singing consistently. I felt as if my facial expressions were more in sync with what I wanted to express than the rest of my body. I also felt my throat get dry. Must remember to have bottled water on hand next time, etc.

Compare your observations with your listener's feedback.

Reward yourself for all the steps you've taken this week toward reaching your intended goal. Think about a "thank-you" token for your listener(s) in appreciation of their time, to be given at the end of the 30-day countdown!

Day 21:

Congratulations! You've made it through the first week and you've worked hard. Reward yourself with a free day. Do something fun and don't think about singing today!

Day 20

Confirm the next mock audition on Day 15 with your audience members.

Back to work! This week you will focus on the mental training needed to maintain your focus. You will strengthen your mental training by tapping into emotions and sensory memory while singing. This work will also help sharpen your focus.

The point of singing is to express the emotional landscape of the music and text. If you approach your character as if meeting a living breathing human being, with normal human functions and needs such as your own, you will be closer to finding the essence of this character in yourself. Your senses and imagination offer a treasure chest full of options for you to explore and use in your interpretation. The more you practice getting in touch with the various emotional impulses and reactions inside of yourself, the more authentic your interpretation will be.

When working on any piece, it is essential that you explore the emotions of the character, as *you* would feel them in a similar situation. In some cases you may have never directly experienced exactly what the character is going through, but you can find many substitutions that would perhaps arouse a similar emotional reaction in you to the one your character is experiencing.

Identifying Attitudes and Emotions

During the following exercises, you will begin to develop your self-awareness. You will begin to become aware of your personal behavior in your daily experiences. You will explore your emotional and sensory memory as they relate to the physical and emotional realities of the character or the text you are singing.

Today we will begin concentrating on triggering your emotional memory.

- Using the answers from your Performance Environment Worksheet, identify the main emotions driving your character in the moment you sing two of your arias.

(See Attitudes and Emotions Chart and Worksheets, p. 164-172)

- Taking the exercise a step further, try to replace your trigger words with an emotional memory of a situation in which you've experienced the same emotion or attitude that the character is experiencing. Once you have recalled the moment and can remember the felt sense associated with it, you are ready to begin singing the aria. (You will learn how to do this in more detail on Day 19.)

- At this point, make sure your recorder is on. Allow yourself to concentrate primarily on the emotional connection to what you're singing. Once you feel comfortable with the emotional connection, try to incorporate the emotion with the technical considerations.

- Take a short break and then repeat the same process with the second aria.

Day 19

Taking yesterday's work a step further, let us concentrate on triggering Sense Memory.

(See Triggering Sense Memory Worksheets, pp. 173-175)

- Using the answers about your character's environment from Day 29's Performance Environment Worksheet, identify the elements that can influence the character's senses.

- Take the same two arias from yesterday's session and identify the elements in your character's environment that trigger each of the five senses: Touch, Smell, Taste, Hearing and Sight.

- Write down the situations that trigger each of the sense memories for you personally and try to recall these situations while singing one of the arias.

- Turn on your recorder. Now, consciously focus upon the situation that triggered the emotion or sense memory and sing the aria through to the point where the sense or emotion changes, if relevant. Then either change the sense memory accordingly or remain in the appropriate situation mentally while singing the entire aria.

- Remember to continue incorporating your shifts in focus. Repeat the aria, varying your sense memories or emotions/attitudes until the aria begins to feel personal, real and spontaneous. Experiment with various physical gestures that are appropriate/organic to the emotion or attitude you are sensing while singing. At this point, it's usually a good idea to begin working in front of a mirror.

Take a break. Before beginning again, center yourself and state your intention. Make sure your recorder is on. Recall your trigger words for the beginning of the aria and sing it through in performance mode. Repeat the process for the second aria.

Accessing your sense memory may prove challenging. In that case, a session or two with an actor, acting instructor or drama coach can be very helpful. Often, movement helps trigger sense memory and expressive freedom. For some, a dance class might prove helpful and freeing.

Day 18

Repeat the work of Day 19 with the remaining two audition arias.

Day 17

Begin your practice session by identifying the sense memory, attitude or emotion you will focus on at the appropriate moments and shifts of focus during your first aria.
Center yourself and state your intentions for this aria.

Sing the aria through in performance mode and note how well you were able to maintain your intended focus.
Repeat the process for each of the remaining three arias, taking a short break between each aria to re-focus and write down your observations. Be sure to include the positive improvements you've noticed.

Day 16

You should plan to practice with your accompanist today.

Write five affirmations for each of your arias. These affirmations should be based on the positive developments you have made since the initial recording. Use the Mock Audition worksheet as well as the feedback you've received to form your affirmations.

(See Aria Affirmations Worksheets, pp. 176-177)

Place the affirmations at your piano, at your bedside, in your music folder, anywhere you are sure to see them throughout the day. Read them aloud in front of a mirror in the morning and aloud in bed before you go to sleep. This process builds your mental muscle and gives you positive self-talk practice.

> ➤ Begin your practice session by warming up to sing in performance mode.

> ➤ Turn on your recorder and leave the room.

> ➤ Read your aria affirmations for the piece you will sing.

> ➤ Center yourself and state your intention. Recall your sense memory and attitude triggers.

> ➤ Take all the time you need. Enter the practice room only when you feel centered and ready.

> ➤ Enter the room and introduce the aria. Fix your focus point on an object or direction below eye level. Create your performance environment and then indicate to your accompanist when you are ready to begin.

> ➤ Sing through the first aria in performance mode.

> ➤ Have your accompanist choose the next aria to be sung.

➢ Take time to recall your affirmations, performance environment and sense trigger words for that aria and indicate when you are ready before beginning. Sing the aria through in performance mode.

➢ Have your accompanist choose the next aria to be sung and repeat above process.

➢ Finally sing the fourth aria in performance mode.

➢ Take a break and discuss with your coach/accompanist anything that needs to be worked on. Write down these points and turn off your recorder.

Day 15: Mock Audition #2

Before the mock audition:

• Begin your session as normal with centering and intending to "nail it" during your mock performance.

• Warm up with the appropriate exercises.

• Be sure to have paper and pens for your audience to write their comments on the feedback sheet you will provide.

At the mock audition:

• Record your arias in performance mode during your mock performance. Center yourself and state your intention to "just do it – nail it!"

- Before entering the room, recall your **aria affirmations**, your **trigger words** and **shifts in focus** for the aria you will sing first.

- Enter the room and announce the first selection.

- Expand your performance environment to include the sensory, attitudes, and emotions work done over the last four days. Decide to "Just do it — nail it!"

- At the end of each aria, immediately concentrate on the environment for the next aria. Don't be tempted to review what you've just done. There will be time for that later. Shift your focus immediately to the next piece, the next person and the emotional and sensory landscape facing you at the present moment. Quickly decide to "just do it – nail it" and sing the next aria.

After the mock audition:

- At the end of the performance, be sure to thank your audience members for their support and get their feedback sheets.

- Make detailed notes after your mock performance as to how you felt before, during and after each aria in terms of the essential T-I-M-E elements of optimal performance.

**(See Mock Audition #2 Observations
Worksheets, pp. 178-182)**

- Make written notes about how you felt the
  performance went for each aria, in detail, in
  terms of the essential T-I-M-E elements
  you've been working on this past week. Be
  detailed and be sure to write the good as
  well as what needs more work. Try to write
  all your observations in a positive vain!

- Compare your observations with the
  feedback from your audience and the
  recording.

Day 14

Congratulations, you are halfway through *Nail Your
Next Audition*!

Today you will rest your voice and work with
visualization exercises or "imaging" your
performance.

*Exercise: "Image" or visualize your performance
as a movie trailer with you in the audience
watching.*

➤ Center

➤ State Intention "to watch yourself perform
  your opening audition aria optimally".

➤ Find visual focal point (stage, crook of the
  piano,…).

> ➤ See yourself walking onto the stage or into the room.

> ➤ Hear and see yourself introducing yourself and your piece.

> ➤ See yourself creating your performance environment, thinking of your trigger words.

> ➤ Imagine your first inhalation, engagement of support muscles and onset of sound.

> ➤ Hear the optimum sound in your imagination and watch your body language.

> ➤ Run through the entire song in performance mode in your inner ear, feel and accept the good feeling of having done 90 % of what you intended.

If you find it difficult to imagine singing the piece from start to finish without interruption, repeat the exercise again and focus on seeing your mental performance in stages.

- Using your shifts in focus as a "cut" command, begin with centering and stating your intention to watch yourself perform the aria in stages, from one shift of focus to the next.

- When you have sung through the various shifts of focus to the end of the aria, return to the beginning of the piece and repeat the process singing through two or three shifts of focus, until you have finished the piece.

- Repeat the process until you have sung through the entire aria without stopping

If you find yourself making mistakes or correcting technical passages while imagining the run-through of the aria:

- Stop immediately after the mistake or break in concentration and go back to just before the problem spot, slow down the tempo and repeat the passage several times, just as you would if practicing aloud.

- Now work it up to tempo. Repeat it in tempo three times.

- Finally return to the beginning of the piece and practice it through to the end, in tempo. See yourself executing the difficult spot perfectly in tempo and singing to the end.

Repeat the exercises above for your remaining arias.

Day 13

1. Warm up.

2. Set up your recorder and turn it on.

3. Leave the room and this time turn up your adrenaline level. You can do this by either running in place for a couple of minutes, doing jumping jacks, or anything that will get your pulse racing. The idea is to simulate a situation where your energy is highly activated, more so

than under any normal performance situation.

4. Immediately begin your centering sequence of concentrating on and regulating your breathing rhythm. Do this for no more than one minute. State your intention to "nail it". Quickly recall two or three trigger words that work best to put you in the performance environment.

5. Enter the room and introduce your aria and sing through in performance mode.

Repeat the process for the remaining four arias, exiting the room each time and activating your adrenaline.

Note how successfully you were able to calm your adrenaline in a timely fashion before having to enter the room and sing on a scale from 1(not successful) to 10 (very successful).

(See Adrenaline Scale Worksheets, pp. 183-184)

Day 12

Re-confirm your mock performance time and place for Day 8. Make sure to remind your support group to plan for various distractions during the mock performance. If at all possible, ask the person(s) listening to your mock performance this week to plan a couple of distractions, which will come up during the performance. Make sure that you are not privy to the details so that you can gauge your reactions from the standpoint of "total surprise".

Working With Distractions

Now you will practice exercises that help you to re-focus immediately upon losing your concentration or eliminate persistent distractions altogether. Today you will begin practicing with distractions added to your practice environment. This is an exercise used by many top seeded athletes as part of their mental training program. It works best when you gradually build the distractions and is especially effective if you engage your support group for help in the element of surprise. Make a list of four or five varying distractions, differing in degree from a bit distracting to extremely distracting. Examples of distractions could include background noise from a stereo or television, an alarm clock, a ringing telephone, a person listening outside the door, people talking in the room or next door, your accompanist playing the wrong tempo or wrong notes, etc. You will use one or more of these distractions during each practice session this week.

> ➢ Decide which distractions you will use today and make sure they are ready to go off. Example: Set your alarm clock to go off well into your practice session and make sure it's in the room with you. Or ask a friend to call your cell phone sometime during your practice session and let it keep ringing or ask the person to keep calling you at various intervals. Maybe add a bowl of tempting snacks in the room or the

television or radio tuned to something a bit annoying.

➢ Center yourself and state your intention to remain in your performance environment in spite of any distractions.

➢ Turn on your recorder.

➢ Warm up using the exercises that you would use in the worst-case scenario.

➢ Begin singing through your audition arias.

➢ If you found it relatively easy to remain focused, try to increase the distractions by layering them or adding new ones – anything that might tempt you to lose focus while in performance mode.

➢ Practice your process goals as usual before moving on to performance mode practice.

➢ When the distraction occurs, be aware of what happens to you physically. Does your adrenaline rise? Does any muscle tension occur? Where? What happened to your concentration? Were you able to regroup and immediately return to your performance environment? If not, what trigger words can you think of to help you recover quickly? Note all of this for later and record it in your Distractions Worksheet.

(See Distractions Worksheet, p. 185)

Day 11

Continue practicing with distractions, but this time, build a boundary around yourself that nothing can penetrate. This boundary is especially important for moments when you are confronted with distractions outside of your control, like uncomfortable chatter, noises, drafts, or other unwelcome things in your sight line within in the hall in which you are singing.

John*, an established singer, was invited to audition for a particular role at a major German opera house. Upon entering the stage, he was distracted by the snickering of one of the auditors. Before he could even get on the stage and introduce himself, he was thrown completely off. He couldn't shake the feeling that this person was snickering about him. As he introduced his aria, all he could think of was the snickering and it stuck with him throughout his audition. Of course, his attention was not where it needed to be and soon he was outside of his performance environment and slowly coming undone. While such a situation is disconcerting, it is exactly one of those examples of distractions outside of your control. Had he been able to immediately build his protective boundary about him, the snickering would have been relegated to its proper place: outside of him, having nothing to do with him and thus not worth his attention. Instead, he chose to make the snickering relevant to him. Gone was his concentration on what was relevant to his performance and hence, the disintegration of his performance.

(See Creating Boundaries, p. 186)

The following exercise is designed to help you build a protection apparatus that allows you to maintain focus, in spite of distractions or adverse situations.

As you sing through your two your arias with the various distractions, choose one of the boundaries from your worksheet and make your intention to stay focused within that boundary, no matter what happens. Repeat the arias with different boundaries or layer them until you feel invincible.

Day 10

Plan to work with your accompanist today.

Continue your work with visualizing your performance, adrenaline stimulation, distractions and boundaries for all four arias. Note what distractions are more difficult to ignore. Perhaps they occur from within, and are not related to outside forces. These are often the most difficult to ignore or keep at bay.

Today, we will explore one more exercise that I have found to be particularly helpful for those types of distractions. I learned this exercise during a session with Alma Thomas (co-author, *Power Performance for Singers*) and it has helped me to delay giving the distraction my attention until a later time. It is called the Magic Box.

(See Magic Box Worksheet, p. 187)

In this exercise, you use the power of your imagination to allow you to put a distraction aside for the time being, with the assurance that you will not ignore it, but will attend to it later when you are more able to focus on it.

If you find yourself with a distraction that is persistent, try putting it your Magic Box. You'll be amazed how powerful this simple little exercise is. The Magic Box becomes a safe repository for what you cannot deal with at the moment and allows you to leave it there for safe keeping until you can.

Day 9

Do not sing today, but rather use your mental imagery for your practice session.

Today, you will practice a thorough mental run-through.

➢ Imagine your warm-up, centering and intention to do all you can to "nail it", no matter what. See yourself surrounded by your boundary, recalling how well you sing your arias and what makes you such a good performer.

➢ Imagine your trigger words for your opening aria.

➢ See yourself enter the room, stand at the piano and announce your opening aria.

➢ See yourself focus your attention on your performance environment trigger words.

➢ Imagine your first inhalation and release of sound. Enjoy the sound you hear. Enjoy watching your intensive focus and shifts in focus along with the various colors and phrasings, which you've worked so hard to execute.

➤ See yourself poised and singing with ease, especially at the technically challenging moments. Hear those phrases being nailed by you, sung exactly as you've practiced them.

➤ Imagine the excited, positive response of your audience.

➤ Imagine calmly waiting to hear what you will be asked to perform next and recreating your performance environment all over again. You are in your flow and singing well. Everything is working together as you would like. You are giving an optimum performance.

Scripting Your Ideal Performance

If you find this mental imaging of your performance difficult, try imagining your favorite singer performing the same aria. See the entire "mental movie" as he/she would likely perform the aria. Slowly replace the face of your model singer with your own. See yourself executing the aria just as he/she would. Be sure to imagine how good singing well makes you feel! Imagine being in control, being in the flow, doing a good job expressing all you wanted to express.

(See Ideal Performance Script, p. 188)

Day 8: Mock Audition #3 with Distractions

Before the mock audition:

- Begin your session as normal with centering and intending to "nail it", no matter what happens during your mock audition.

- Warm up with the appropriate exercises.

- Be sure to have paper and pens for your audience to write down feedback.

At the mock audition:

- Record your arias in performance mode during your mock performance. Center yourself and state your intention to "just do it - nail it!"

- Before entering the room, build your protective boundary around you. No distractions will be allowed within your boundary. Within your boundary, recall the surge of energy your mental run-through gave you yesterday. Recall how good it felt to be able to do all you had worked to do. Recall one or two trigger words for your first aria's performance environment.

- Enter the room and announce the first selection.

- Resolve to remain anchored within your boundary, oblivious to what happens outside of it.

- At the end of your opening aria, calmly wait for the request for the next aria and then immediately concentrate on the environment for that aria. Resolve to do all you can to "nail it" again, no matter what. If for any reason, some unwanted distraction enters your boundary, continue in performance mode, quickly recalling another trigger word or the same one. Think only of where you are in the moment and resist the temptation to consider what went on previously. Continue this process, regardless of the distractions coming at you. It will get easier as you go along.

After the mock audition:

- At the end of the performance, be sure to thank your audience members for their support and get their feedback sheets.

- Make detailed notes after your mock performance as to how you felt before, during and after each aria in terms of the essential T-I-M-E elements of optimal performance.

(See Mock Audition #3 Observations Worksheets, pp. 189-193)

- Make written notes about how you felt the performance went for each aria, in detail, in terms of distractions thrown at you and those you may have allowed to surface from within. Be detailed and be sure to write what was good as well as what needs more work.

Try to write all your observations in a positive vein!

- Compare your observations with the feedback from your audience and the recording.

Dos and Don'ts Leading Up to Audition Day

Congratulations! You've reached the home stretch of *Nail Your Next Audition.* Can you feel the excitement?

The final week of the 30-day countdown will ideally culminate in an actual audition. If you have no opportunity to do an actual audition, make an audition recording, which you will use to send out with your materials for competitions or auditions requiring one. This recording can also be used as an introduction of your singing to send to various agents or conductors.

If you make the audition recording, it must be done in one take, without repeating or correcting. You could also set up your own performance audition by inviting friends and family as well as your supporters and mentors.

If you have an audition set up for a future date, be sure to continue practicing the exercises, refining your goals and updating your performance and aria trigger words in the days prior to your audition.

This week will be focused more on energy conservation so that you will have an optimal amount of physical and vocal strength on the big day. You will do a lot less actual singing this week and concentrate much more on the mental fortitude you need for optimum performance.

1. DO use all the positive images at your disposal. See, hear yourself doing well, singing confidently, building your performance environment and staying within it, repeating your performance and aria affirmations, reminding yourself of your assets with positive self-talk. You need to convince yourself that you are going to perform the way you intend to and that all the work you've done over the past three weeks will help you do just that. Remember that your mental attitude is the key to performing well at your audition.

2. DO NOT pressure yourself to be perfect or better than ever. Aim for singing as good as your 90 % or better, but don't go for 100 %. The pressure to do better than ever will undoubtedly take your attention away from the process of doing just "well". Your "extra" efforts will potentially take your mind out of the familiar realm of doing just what you need to do.

3. DO get lots of rest, both vocal and physical. Sleep is very important at this stage for concentration and recovery. Get at least 8 hours a night. Do more mental practicing than actual singing this week. Your vocal cords will thank you by being fresh and pliable for the actual audition. Your body will respond to you by being strong, fit and energized, giving the extra physical support your voice needs.

4. DO NOT sing too much. Use more mental practice techniques such as those worked last week. Conserve your energy by only practicing

what absolutely needs to be practiced and do so at the same time of day your audition is scheduled for. Resist the temptation to sing through your arias the day before your audition. Mentally running through your arias is more effective at this point than singing them. Your brain receives impulses from your mere thoughts that "exercise" your muscles "as if" you were actually physically singing.

5. DO plan your audition wardrobe and pack your audition bag. If the audition is out of town, make sure you have what you need for a good night's sleep (ear plugs, warm pajamas, nose or throat spray, meds for emergencies like sinus infections or sore throats, a good umbrella, etc.). Pack your bottled water or juice, a snack, your affirmation and trigger word sheets, music for the accompanist, venue address, and extra pantyhose). If anything needs to go to the cleaners, make sure it will be ready a few days before your audition. In general, prepare all that you think you will need to have with you the day of your audition.

6. DO NOT drink alcohol or eat heavy meals late at night. Heavy late meals put an extra burden on your digestive system while you're sleeping. This can disturb your sleep patterns. Alcohol dehydrates the body and especially the vocal cords and decreases your energy and concentration levels.

7. DO find pleasant and low energy distractions like a short walk outdoors, a good movie (preferably something light or funny), reading a good book at a nice café, etc.

8. DO NOT fill your schedule with unnecessary appointments, meetings or anything that can wait until after the audition. This includes meeting friends in situations where you will have to talk too much or be surrounded by lots of people, smoke, or germs. This is the time to be more with yourself, to build your boundaries and to concentrate only upon what you need in order to do well.

DAY 7

Today, begin by centering yourself and formulating your intention for audition day.

(See Audition Day Intention Worksheet, p. 194)

➤ Begin food intake and sleep routine log.

(See Daily Routine Log, pp. 195-200)

This week, it is important to get at least 7 hours sleep each night. Rest is the biggest secret to performing optimally! Be sure to watch what you eat and to stick to the routine all week.

➤ Make a list of essentials that you will need to take with you to the audition venue. Make sure to check it off as you pack your bag.

(See Audition Needs Worksheet p. 201)

➤ Prepare an Emergency Contingency Plan **(See ECP Worksheet, p. 202)**, that includes emergency warm-up, affirmations, positive self-talk, trigger words, curbing or pumping adrenaline, etc. for use in the case of unexpected distractions, loss of concentration, or nervous energy. These are the words or routines that work under the most extreme circumstances, instantaneously and without the need of much effort, concentration, time or preparation.

➤ Plan and prepare your audition wardrobe. This is the time to do any washing, ironing, trips to the cleaners, or last minute shopping. Make sure your shoes are polished, clothes are mended or altered if needed. Try on your audition wardrobe. Consider consulting someone you trust to have a look and offer any suggestions.

(See Audition Wardrobe Do's and Don'ts, pp. 203-205)

A special note about the accompanist's music:

• Make sure that you help yourself, by providing your accompanist with a fully legible and easy to read copy of your music.
• If using an original score make sure that the pages turn easily and that the binding has been broken in.
• If using copied music, make sure that all of the notes are legible and that the pages turn easily.
• Make sure cuts are clearly marked or covered with paper.

- Make sure to clearly mark your dynamics, tempi and any other important information not already in the score.
- Do not place your sheets of music in individual plastic covers as this can produce excessive glare from the lights.
- Do not give your pianist loose or stapled sheets of music.

DAY 6

Begin your practice with imagining your vocal warm-up. Imagine singing the exercises you normally use when you have a lot of time to warm-up and are feeling well. Center yourself and intend to "nail it" today. Now, actually warm-up using the exercises you'd use when you have little time. These are the exercises you identified as being the ones that warm up your voice quickest. There should be no more than three or four short ones.

Today, practice your opening aria and the most difficult piece in performance mode and *in your audition clothes*. Afterwards, make any adjustments to your wardrobe if necessary.

DAY 5

Today you will assess your progress toward the goals you intended to reach. You will assess any improvements you've made in your arias and in your overall performance skills. Throughout today's session, be vigilant in your positive energy, and positive self-talk. This is normally the time when self-doubt rises. Don't panic! This is normal, but now you have the tools to redirect the negative energy to the positive. Concentrate on the progress and improvements noted by your support group and yourself.

➢ Take out your Day 30 Initial Recording, the Mock Audition 1, 2, and 3 recordings as well as the Aria Assessment Worksheet with your ultimate goals. Listen to the initial recording and then to the Mock Auditions. Re-read your notations made after each mock performance, as well as the feedback sheets from your listeners.

➢ Using the Goals Assessment sheet, compare how close you've come to reaching your ultimate goal during each mock audition. Base your opinions upon the feedback you've received in addition to your own post mock audition observations and the observations you made during today's listening session.

(See Goals Assessment Worksheets, pp. 206-207)

➢ Based on what you've achieved or improved during the last 3 weeks, make a final list of performance affirmations, which you will take with you to the audition.

(See Final Affirmations Worksheet, p. 208)

➢ Revisit your Magic Box and try to resolve any lingering distractions.

DAY 4

You will need your pianist today.

If at all possible, try to arrange to visit the audition venue before your audition day. If possible, get a feel for the room and the acoustics. Stand next to the piano and imagine yourself singing pretty well and being happy with your performance overall. If you can sing through your opening aria, do so. If not, take in the space visually. Imagine your voice filling the space beautifully and effortlessly.

If a visit is not possible, try to arrange to practice in a different space with a different acoustic today. Practice for only one half hour.

> ➢ Center yourself and warm-up using the worst-case scenario exercises. Intend to "nail it" no matter what.

> ➢ Recall the final trigger words for your opening aria, surround yourself with your protective boundary and enter the room.

> ➢ Announce your aria and create your performance environment before beginning to sing.

> ➢ Begin another aria, but don't sing it through to the end.

> ➢ In the third and fourth aria, choose to sing a section from each.

➤ End your singing session.

➤ Based upon this practice session, make your Final Aria Trigger Words, limiting yourself to only one word or phrase for each aria.

(See Final Aria Trigger Words Worksheet, pp. 209)

DAY 3

Today you will sing through sections of your arias, concentrating on shifts of focus.

Begin only one bar or phrase before a shift of focus and sing through to the end of the phrase only. Do this for each aria.

Repeat your final performance affirmations in a mirror. Remember, these affirmations are based upon the recorded proof of your mock auditions and the honest feedback from your support group as well as your own observations. They are very real observations about what you have already achieved or executed optimally!

At end of your practice session, it is very important to accept your performance for what it is at this moment. Hopefully you've been able to achieve all of your performance goals up to now. If not, the most important thing to concentrate on is what improvements you *have* made and which goals you *have* achieved. Now you must focus on using what you have in this moment to perform well.

> *"Don't let what you cannot do get in the way of what you CAN do!"* Steven Cole, *Tenor*

DAY 2

NO SINGING

Today your practice session will consist only of **mental run-throughs** of your arias.
Read through your score for any reminders and incorporate them into your mental run-through.

Do a mental run-through of your entire performance from start to finish. This time, include your arrival at the audition venue. See yourself entering the room, perhaps filled with other singers. Imagine yourself being friendly, but detached. See yourself going over your affirmations in your mind, your trigger words, centering yourself and resolving to "nail it" before entering the room. See yourself facing various distractions by constructing your protective boundary. See yourself remaining poised and confident. If your energy feels too low, see yourself pumping up your adrenaline. If your energy is too high, see yourself centering your breathing.

Take a nice walk in the fresh air. See a movie or read a good book. Check your audition wardrobe one last time. Get a good night's sleep.

Day 1: NAIL YOUR AUDITION!

Congratulations on making it to the BIG DAY!
This is the day when all of your hard work and
efforts will pay off in a big way. Today you will
nail your audition. Here's why:

> ➤ You've hung in there for four weeks,
> setting, refining and working toward
> your goals, preparing yourself mentally
> by improving and consciously directing
> your attention and focus.

> ➤ You've done the audition three times
> already, each time with more and more
> progress in controlling your skills.

> ➤ You've worked to improve your self-talk
> and concentrate on the positive elements
> of your singing.

> ➤ You've gone within and listened to your
> inner voice, the power in you that knows
> how to achieve all your goals and
> dreams. Now is the moment when you
> TRUST. Trust that you know what you
> have to do and how to do it. Trust that
> your work has been productive and the
> reward will be your ability to perform
> just as well for the real thing as you have
> in your practice sessions and mock
> audition situations.

When you awaken, before getting out of bed, center yourself. Go within and remind yourself why you sing. Recall the positive effects your voice has on the audience and on yourself. Recall your final performance affirmations and repeat them quietly to yourself. State your intention: to do everything you've been practicing for the last four weeks today – nothing more and nothing less.

Stick to your plan! Keep your eye on the prize.

Begin your day with the same routine as the last six days. Do not make any variations!

Before going to the venue, re-check your audition needs bag. Check it against your list. Make sure it includes:
- Music for the accompanist
- Bottled water or juice and a snack
- Emergency contingency plan
- Final affirmations
- Aria trigger words
- Warm-up exercises for every occasion
- List of goals achieved and improvements made.

Warm up using your optimum/ideal warm-up exercises.

On your way to the audition venue, run your movie again from the moment you enter the venue until you finish singing.

➢ As you enter the audition venue, surround yourself with your personal boundary. It will serve you well from the moment you enter the building until you leave.

➤ Keep your list of affirmations handy in case you have lots of time on your hands.

➤ If you feel nervous energy creeping in, immediately center yourself and your breathing, read your affirmations or focus upon your list of what you do really well. Remind yourself to keep breathing deeply. It may help to take your mind completely off the situation you are in by reading something or thinking about something totally unrelated to your audition. For many, it helps to go over the performance in their minds. In extreme cases, read over your Emergency Contingency Plan.

Step Into Your Spotlight

Your time is *now*. You are ready for it. You know how. You've done it countless times in the last four weeks. This is no different! In fact, it's routine for you!

1. State your intention.

2. Center quickly and regulate your breathing.

3. Decide to do your best to "nail it", no matter what.

4. Recall your performance trigger words or affirmations.

5. Establish your boundary.

6. Enter the room, announce your first selection, create your performance environment and begin!

7. Remain calm and poised as you wait for the next request, if there is one.

8. Immediately re-group and concentrate upon the trigger words for the next aria. You've done it before and will do it again now. Remain in the moment, and resist thinking about what went on previously. Think only of expressing all there is in you at this time, for the aria you are about to sing.

9. Thank your auditors and exit.

10. Feel the excitement of having succeeded in singing well under the toughest of circumstances. Reward yourself for a job well done. Enjoy and celebrate!

After The Audition

Evaluate Your Audition Performance

A day or two after the audition, it is very
important to record your observations of how it
all went. Describe on the Audition Evaluation
Sheet your overall impressions about how well
you were able to remain focused, create your
performance environment, recall helpful tools
for concentration, etc. In the two columns
provided, write what went well and what didn't.
Write down what you think would help you to
improve what didn't go as well as you would
have liked. Alma Thomas and Shirley Emmons
advocate crossing out or cutting out and
throwing away the negatives comments of your
experience once you've considered them.
(*Power Performance For Singers,* 1998) Save
the positive comments for later reflection prior
to your next audition.

**(See Audition Evaluation Worksheets, pp.
210-211)**

Afterword

Remember that the more you continue to incorporate the exercises for the all essential T-I-M-E elements of optimal performance into your daily practice, the easier it will be to recall them at will.

Whether or not you actually get the job is based on many reasons, many of which are completely outside of your control. The only thing you can control is how well you plan your T-I-M-E to step into your spotlight during the audition and give the listeners all the L-O-V-E you have to give. If you have achieved this, you have nailed your audition!

Countdown Worksheets

Intention Revelation Worksheets

In a quiet moment, close your eyes and take several slow, deep breaths. Continue until your breathing pattern slows to a relaxed and peaceful pace. Now imagine yourself at a moment in the near future. You are happy and enjoying yourself. Take a closer look at yourself and your environment and answer the following questions.

1. What has made you so happy and content?

2. What is your life about?

3. How does a typical day in your life look?

4. How do you interact with the other people in your life?

Intention Revelation Worksheets continued

5. What have you accomplished or achieved?

6. How have you grown?

7. What have you learned about yourself?

8. What are you looking forward to in the
    future?

Intended Accomplishment Worksheet

Using the answers from the Intention Revelation Worksheet, begin to formulate what you intend to accomplish in your life.

1. What do you really want?

2. Why do you want it?

3. What will be the outcome of having what you want?

4. What will it mean to you and your life?

5. Describe how you will *feel* once you have what you really want.

Intended Accomplishment Worksheets
continued

Savor the feeling you have described. Return to this feeling frequently in your quiet moments for at least 5 minutes everyday.

Reinforce the feeling and life you have imagined with corresponding pictures from magazines, publicity materials from various opera or concert houses and recording companies with your name added to the cast list, artist development department or agent rosters, etc. Use your imagination and have fun creating your "intended" world. See and describe it in detail.

Clear From Fear Worksheets

This exercise is adapted from Dr. Eugene T.
Gendlin's book, *Focusing,* 1978. Dr. Gendlin
developed the technique of "Focusing" which is in
essence, "...a process in which you make contact
with a special kind of internal bodily awareness...a
felt sense." (*Focusing,* 1978)

A "felt sense" is initially a vague physical
awareness of a particular problem or situation
which then slowly comes into focus and eventually
changes.

"When your felt sense changes, *you change* – and,
therefore, so does your life."(*Focusing,* p. 32)

Remember, a felt sense is not an emotion, but rather
a body sense of something meaningful that needs
your attention.

There are six steps to focusing. This process
awakens body awareness and through this
awareness, a physical shift or change in the body
that also affects a shift or change in your
perspective. In other words, your problem,
experienced as a felt sense that shifts, seems
different and is often solved. The body awareness
works to release your problems, blocks and fears.
Try focusing whenever you feel yourself blocked or
unable to move forward toward your goals.

Prepare to Focus.

Clear From Fear Worksheets continued

Find a time and space to sit quietly for a while
without interruptions. Have your **Clear the Fear**
worksheet and a pen handy. Make sure you are
warm enough and comfortable. Relax physically
and mentally.

Step 1
Begin with an awareness of your intended
accomplishment. Begin to sense any blocks or fears
that seem to be on the path before you. As they
occur to you, make a mental note of them, like
making a shopping list. Try to remain detached
from them. When you feel sure that you've
acknowledged all that has come to mind and are
comfortable having done that, it's time to move to
the next step.

Step 2
Ask yourself which of the problems on your list
feels the most overwhelming right now. If you
can't differentiate between them, simply choose one
to direct your attention to. As you consider this
problem, block or fear, begin to observe your body
and the way it *feels*. Ask yourself what does the
problem *feel* like. Without answering the question
in words, feel the whole problem and the sense of
all that it is. Turn off the self-talk and avoid
analyzing the problem. Just observe how you feel in
your body as you sit with the problem. Try to get a
sense of a single feeling located somewhere in your
body that calls your attention to it. It can, and most
probably will be very subtle or vague. Maybe it is a

Clear From Fear Worksheets continued

tight feeling in your throat or a queasy feeling in your stomach. It could be a quickening of your breath or take the form of feeling constricted, on the verge of tears, a tightness, heaviness, expansion, blankness, peacefulness, emptyness or something else. Without judging, analyzing or trying to fix it, silently acknowledge that you know it is there and just sit with the felt sense of your problem for a while.

What do you want to focus on?

Where do you sense this problem in your body?

What does it feel like?

"In seeking the felt sense of a problem, you are trying to make your mind do essentially what it does when calling up the feeling of your sense of a person." (*Focusing*, p. 54)

Step 3
How would you describe the felt sense? Find a word, phrase, image, sound or gesture that comes closest to describing the core of your felt sense. If something in your felt sense stirs or moves, intensifies or releases as you begin to describe it, you are on the right track. Take your time and stay with the feeling until you find a description that resonates within you and *feels* just right. When this occurs, you will generally feel the "aha " effect.

Clear From Fear Worksheets continued

Something has shifted in you. Something about the felt sense has begun to change.

What words, phrases, images or other descriptions come to mind when you focus on the felt sense?

What description feels just right?

Step 4
Check the description you found to be closest to your felt sense and check it again with the feeling in your body. Does it still resonate? Ask yourself if it is right and then feel whether or not it is. If it is, you will feel some sort of shift in your body. It may be a deep breath, a sense of release or a sigh that let's you know the description is just right. If this doesn't happen, go back to the felt sense itself and experience feeling it anew. Repeat the process of allowing the right description to come to you as you sit with the felt sense. Take your time and be patient. This is all part of the process of effecting change and clearing the path to your success.

Step 5
If you have experienced a shift or release in your body, speak directly to your described felt sense and ask what it is, needs, wants. For instance, if your description of your felt sense of tightness in your throat is "choked off", ask the felt sense what it is

Clear From Fear Worksheets continued

about your problem that makes you feel so "choked off". After you ask the question, avoid trying to answer it intellectually or mentally. In fact most of the answers that come to you quickly are just your brain responding and not your body. Let them just go by and after sensing into your felt sense, ask it again, what is it about this problem that chokes off your felt sense. Or simply ask it what it needs in order to not feel so choked off. Again, avoid rushing to force quick answers. Take your time and your body will reward you with a clear feeling of release, well being and deeper understanding of what you need to do to help it release the problem. It may take more than one session to get to the core of the felt sense. In that case, stop the session and come back to it again at another time.

What about your problem makes you feel so...

What does your felt sense need in order to feel okay with the problem?

Clear From Fear Worksheets continued

Step 6
Welcome whatever has come to you during your focusing session. Receive it as you would a gift from a good friend. You don't have to like it or agree with it, but just accept it graciously. It is a precious gift that will keep on giving as you continue to explore your fears and face them. Jot down all of your impressions from your focusing session.

Repeat the process for any other blocks you encounter on the path to your intended accomplishment.

My Intention Statement

At the conclusion of *Nail Your Next Audition, The Ultimate 30-Day Guide For Singers*, I, _____, intend to accomplish the following:

Signature_____

Date_____

My Personal Best Assessment Worksheets

Recall in as much detail as possible a performance
or moments in a performance where you achieved
your personal best. Describe what being "in the
flow of the moment" felt like.

What did it feel like to be in the flow of the
performance?

What sensation or emotions did performing well
activate?

How did your body feel while singing? Before
singing? After singing?

Describe the sound, texture, and timbre of your
voice. Describe how it felt while singing and how it
sounded in your ear.

**My Personal Best Assessment Worksheets
continued**

How did the space around you feel? How did you
feel in the space? In your body?

What pictures or words come close to describing the
experience, the way you sang, your relationship to
those on stage with you, etc.?

What did you do to prepare? What was your
routine on the day of the performance?

What was your energy stimulation like on a scale of
1(sluggish) to 10 (manic)?

Performance Affirmations Worksheet

Write a list of positive statements of fact, in the present tense, describing your abilities and qualities as a singer and performer. (Refer to *Nail Your Next Audition*, p. 21)

1. _____

2. _____

3. _____

4. _____

5. _____

6. _____

7. _____

8. _____

9. _____

10. _____

Warm Up Exercises for Every Occasion

Ideal: Perfect conditions, vocally and physically fit

    1. _____

    2. _____

    3. _____

    4. _____

Quick: Exercises that warm your voice up quickly

    1. _____

    2. _____

    3. _____

    4. _____

Worst Case: Exercises for fatigue, anxiety, illness

    1. _____

    2. _____

    3. _____

    4. _____

Initial Recording Observations Worksheets

Write down your observations and impressions of your over all performance **before** listening to the initial recording. Recall what it felt like as you were singing the arias and describe how you perceived your performance in the moment you were singing. What went well? What did not go well? Note any body tension, how well you concentrated, your ability to recover quickly in the case of mistakes, and any negative self-talk or emotions that occurred.

Overall Performance Impressions:

Initial Recording Observations Worksheets

Specific Impressions:

Aria 1
Title_____

Aria 2
Title_____

Aria 3
Title_____

Aria 4
Title_____

Initial Recording Aria Assessment Worksheets

On a scale of 1 (not at all present) to 10 (consistently present), rate how successfully you performed each of your arias in terms of the essential **T-I-M-E-** elements of optimal performance. The numbers represent the percentage of effectiveness in each area.

Initial Recording

Aria 1
Title_____

Technical Proficiency:
Consider vocal quality and timbre, diction, dynamics, phrasing, pitch and rhythmic accuracy, overall technical and musical skills.

1   2   3   4   5   6   7   8   9   10

Comments:
What did you do well technically ?

What needs work technically? List specific vocal exercises, body tension release exercises, etc. you can use to improve.

Initial Recording Aria Assessments continued

Aria 1
Title_____

Inner Awareness:
Consider whether your joy or commitment to singing is
evident. Is there a sense of confidence coming through in
your sound? Are you expressing text or merely singing
words? How effective are you in communicating what you
have to say in this aria? Is body tension or negative self-talk in
your way? How did you feel while singing?

1   2   3   4   5   6   7   8   9   10

Comments:
What did you do well in communicating your inner awareness
of why you're singing this aria? Were you able to recognize
and release tension or negative self-talk?

What needs work in helping to communicate why you're
singing this aria? What could you do to improve in this area?
What needs your focus?

Initial Recording Aria Assessments continued

Aria 1
Title_____

Mental Muscle:
Consider how well you were able to focus your attention.
How much of the time were you able to flow between
concentrated vs. passive focus?   How successful were you in
re-directing your focus when distractions or mistakes
interrupted your concentration? How successful were you in
directing your thoughts and controlling your self-talk
throughout the piece?

1   2   3   4   5   6   7   8   9   10

Comments:
In what ways did your mental muscle help you during the
aria?

What do you need to work on in order to build and train your
mental muscle? How much time will you need to devote to
this training?

Initial Recording Aria Assessments continued

Aria 1
Title_____

Expressive Freedom:

Consider how successfully did you use your technical skills to express the dramatic situation of your character. How successfully did you in communicate your understanding and feelings about what your character's physical and emotional situation? How much of the time can you *hear* the emotions you are interpreting?

1   2   3   4   5   6   7   8   9   10

Comments:

What emotions or dramatic situations did you successfully communicate through the sound of your voice?

What emotions or dramatic situations would you like to be able to communicate through the sound of your voice? How could you improve your abilities in this regard?

Initial Recording Aria Assessments continued

Aria 2
Title_____

Technical Proficiency:
Consider vocal quality and timbre, diction, dynamics,
phrasing, pitch and rhythmic accuracy, overall technical and
musical skills.

1   2   3   4   5   6   7   8   9   10

Comments:
What did you do well technically ?

What needs work technically? List specific vocal exercises,
body tension release exercises, etc. you can use to improve.

Initial Recording Aria Assessments continued

Aria 2
Title_____

Inner Awareness:

Consider whether your joy or commitment to singing is
evident. Is there a sense of confidence coming through in
your sound? Are you expressing text or merely singing
words? How effective are you in communicating what you
have to say in this aria? Is body tension or negative self-talk in
your way? How did you feel while singing?

1   2   3   4   5   6   7   8   9   10

Comments:

What did you do well in communicating your inner awareness
of why you're singing this aria? Were you able to recognize
and release tension or negative self-talk?

What needs work in helping to communicate why you're
singing this aria? What could you do to improve in this area?
What needs your focus?

Initial Recording Aria Assessments continued

Aria 2
Title_____

Mental Muscle:

Consider how well you were able to focus your attention.
How much of the time were you able to flow between
concentrated vs. passive focus?   How successful were you in
re-directing your focus when distractions or mistakes
interrupted your concentration? How successful were you in
directing your thoughts and controlling your self-talk
throughout the piece?

1   2   3   4   5   6   7   8   9   10

Comments:

In what ways did your mental muscle help you during the
aria?

What do you need to work on in order to build and train your
mental muscle? How much time will you need to devote to
this training?

Initial Recording Aria Assessments continued

Aria 2

Title_____

Expressive Freedom:

Consider how successfully did you use your technical skills to express the dramatic situation of your character. How successfully did you in communicate your understanding and feelings about what your character's physical and emotional situation? How much of the time can you *hear* the emotions you are interpreting?

1   2   3   4   5   6   7   8   9   10

Comments:

What emotions or dramatic situations did you successfully communicate through the sound of your voice?

What emotions or dramatic situations would you like to be able to communicate through the sound of your voice? How could you improve your abilities in this regard?

Initial Recording Aria Assessments continued

Aria 3

Title_____

Technical Proficiency:
Consider vocal quality and timbre, diction, dynamics,
phrasing, pitch and rhythmic accuracy, overall technical and
musical skills.

1   2   3   4   5   6   7   8   9   10

Comments:
What did you do well technically ?

What needs work technically? List specific vocal exercises,
body tension release exercises, etc. you can use to improve.

Initial Recording Aria Assessments continued

Aria 3
Title_____

Inner Awareness:
Consider whether your joy or commitment to singing is
evident. Is there a sense of confidence coming through in
your sound? Are you expressing text or merely singing
words? How effective are you in communicating what you
have to say in this aria? Is body tension or negative self-talk in
your way? How did you feel while singing?

1   2   3   4   5   6   7   8   9   10

Comments:
What did you do well in communicating your inner awareness
of why you're singing this aria? Were you able to recognize
and release tension or negative self-talk?

What needs work in helping to communicate why you're
singing this aria? What could you do to improve in this area?
What needs your focus?

Initial Recording Aria Assessments continued

Aria 3
Title_____

Mental Muscle:
Consider how well you were able to focus your attention.
How much of the time were you able to flow between
concentrated vs. passive focus?   How successful were you in
re-directing your focus when distractions or mistakes
interrupted your concentration? How successful were you in
directing your thoughts and controlling your self-talk
throughout the piece?

1   2   3   4   5   6   7   8   9   10

Comments:
In what ways did your mental muscle help you during the
aria?

What do you need to work on in order to build and train your
mental muscle? How much time will you need to devote to
this training?

Initial Recording Aria Assessments continued

Aria 3
Title_____

Expressive Freedom:
Consider how successfully did you use your technical skills to express the dramatic situation of your character. How successfully did you in communicate your understanding and feelings about what your character's physical and emotional situation? How much of the time can you *hear* the emotions you are interpreting?

1   2   3   4   5   6   7   8   9   10

Comments:
What emotions or dramatic situations did you successfully communicate through the sound of your voice?

What emotions or dramatic situations would you like to be able to communicate through the sound of your voice? How could you improve your abilities in this regard?

Initial Recording Aria Assessments continued

Aria 4

Title_____

Technical Proficiency:

Consider vocal quality and timbre, diction, dynamics, phrasing, pitch and rhythmic accuracy, overall technical and musical skills.

1   2   3   4   5   6   7   8   9   10

Comments:

What did you do well technically ?

What needs work technically? List specific vocal exercises, body tension release exercises, etc. you can use to improve.

Initial Recording Aria Assessments continued

Aria 4
Title_____

Inner Awareness:
Consider whether your joy or commitment to singing is
evident. Is there a sense of confidence coming through in
your sound? Are you expressing text or merely singing
words? How effective are you in communicating what you
have to say in this aria? Is body tension or negative self-talk in
your way? How did you feel while singing?

1   2   3   4   5   6   7   8   9   10

Comments:
What did you do well in communicating your inner awareness
of why you're singing this aria? Were you able to recognize
and release tension or negative self-talk?

What needs work in helping to communicate why you're
singing this aria? What could you do to improve in this area?
What needs your focus?

Initial Recording Aria Assessments continued

Aria 4
Title_____

Mental Muscle:

Consider how well you were able to focus your attention.
How much of the time were you able to flow between
concentrated vs. passive focus?   How successful were you in
re-directing your focus when distractions or mistakes
interrupted your concentration? How successful were you in
directing your thoughts and controlling your self-talk
throughout the piece?

1   2   3   4   5   6   7   8   9   10

Comments:

In what ways did your mental muscle help you during the
aria?

What do you need to work on in order to build and train your
mental muscle? How much time will you need to devote to
this training?

Initial Recording Aria Assessments continued

Aria 4
Title_____

Expressive Freedom:
Consider how successfully did you use your technical skills to express the dramatic situation of your character. How successfully did you in communicate your understanding and feelings about what your character's physical and emotional situation? How much of the time can you *hear* the emotions you are interpreting?

1 2 3 4 5 6 7 8 9 10

Comments:
What emotions or dramatic situations did you successfully communicate through the sound of your voice?

What emotions or dramatic situations would you like to be able to communicate through the sound of your voice? How could you improve your abilities in this regard?

30-Day Aria Goals Worksheets

Write down your ultimate goals for each aria. Then write down action goals to help you achieve the ultimate goals. Identify exercises, trigger words or phrases and other tools and techniques that you will use with your action goals. Refer to your Initial Recording Aria Assessment Worksheet for inspiration.

Example:

Aria: Ach ich fühl's

Technical Proficiency

Ultimate Goal:
To float the high B-flat on „Liebe"

Action Goals for Week 1
1. To float the high B-flat I will use the following exercises in my daily practice:

   a. Imagine the vowel falling lower in my body as I ascend into my upper register.

   b. Vocalise for modifying the [i] vowel: 1-5-1, ascending in half steps.

   c. Vowel modification exercise on same vocalise going from [i] to [ü].

30-Day Aria Goals Worksheets continued

2. Relieve any unwanted tension in my jaw, tongue or neck with following exercises:

    a. Imagine the back of my neck long or tall as I approach the interval on
    b. "Liebe"
    c. Imagine a sigh of air going through my nose as I approach the B-flat
    d. Arpeggios on "Yausa" 1-3-5-8-5-3-1 and extended arpeggios 1-3-5-8-10-8-5-3-1

3. Tools, Triggers and Routines to Employ:
    a. Imagery
    b. Tension Release

4. Trigger Words:

    a. "Easy"
    b. "Float"
    c. "Gently Stretch"

Practice exercises 10 minutes at a time, every day for a week. At the end of the 10-minute period, incorporate the work in the phrase leading up to the high B-flat. Practice incorporating my various trigger word at various places before the phrase until I find the combination that gives me the result I want or at least brings me closest to my ideal sound.

Using the above example, make goals for each of the T-I-M-E elements in all four audition arias.

30-Day Aria Goals Worksheets continued

Be sure to plan realistic goals for the end of each week. Try not to overload your weekly schedule. One or two goals per T-I-M-E element is sufficient per week.

End of Week Evaluation:

At the end of each week, evaluate how much progress you've made with your action goals toward your ultimate goals. Decide if any adjustments are necessary or if you think you should continue in the same way. Discuss your goals and evaluation with your voice teacher and coach.

30-Day Aria Goals

Before beginning, make three separate copies of these pages for updating your evaluation after weeks 2, 3 and 4.

Set goals for each of the essential T-I-M-E elements.

Aria 1 Title: _____

Technical Proficiency

Ultimate Goal:

Action Goals:

Tools and Routines:

Week _ Evaluation:

30-Day Aria Goals continued

Aria 1 Title: : _____

Inner Awareness

Ultimate Goal:

Action Goals:

Tools and Routines:

Week _ Evaluation:

30-Day Aria Goals continued

Aria 1 Title:_____

Mental Muscle

Ultimate Goal:

Action Goals:

Tools and Routines:

Week _ Evaluation:

30-Day Aria Goals continued

Aria 1 Title: _____

Expressive Freedom

Ultimate Goal:

Action Goals:

Tools and Routines:

Week _ Evaluation:

30-Day Aria Goals

Before beginning, make three separate copies of these pages for update and evaluation after weeks 2, 3 and 4.

Set goals for each of the essential T-I-M-E elements.

Aria 2 Title: _____

Technical Proficiency

Ultimate Goal:

Action Goals:

Tools and Routines:

Week _ Evaluation:

30-Day Aria Goals continued

Aria 2 Title: _____

Inner Awareness

Ultimate Goal:

Action Goals:

Tools and Routines:

Week _ Evaluation:

30-Day Aria Goals continued

Aria 2 Title: _____

Mental Muscle

Ultimate Goal:

Action Goals:

Tools and Routines:

Week _ Evaluation:

30-Day Aria Goals continued

Aria 2 Title: _____

Expressive Freedom

Ultimate Goal:

Action Goals:

Tools and Routines:

Week _ Evaluation:

30-Day Aria Goals

Before beginning, make three separate copies of these pages for update and evaluation after weeks 2, 3 and 4.

Set goals for each of the essential T-I-M-E elements.

Aria 3 Title: _____

Technical Proficiency

Ultimate Goal:

Action Goals:

Tools and Routines:

Week _ Evaluation:

30-Day Aria Goals continued

Aria 3 Title: _____

Inner Awareness

Ultimate Goal:

Action Goals:

Tools and Routines:

Week _ Evaluation:

30-Day Aria Goals continued

Aria 3 Title: _____

Mental Muscle

Ultimate Goal:

Action Goals:

Tools and Routines:

Week _ Evaluation:

30-Day Aria Goals continued

Aria 3 Title: _____

Expressive Freedom

Ultimate Goal:

Action Goals:

Tools and Routines:

Week _ Evaluation:

30-Day Aria Goals

Before beginning, make three separate copies of these pages for update and evaluation after weeks 2, 3 and 4.

Set goals for each of the essential T-I-M-E elements.

Aria 4 Title: _____

Technical Proficiency

Ultimate Goal:

Action Goals:

Tools and Routines:

Week _ Evaluation:

30-Day Aria Goals continued

Aria 4 Title: _____

Inner Awareness

Ultimate Goal:

Action Goals:

Tools and Routines:

Week _ Evaluation:

30-Day Aria Goals continued

Aria 4 Title: _____

Mental Muscle

Ultimate Goal:

Action Goals:

Tools and Routines:

Week _ Evaluation:

30-Day Aria Goals continued

Aria 4 Title: _____

Expressive Freedom

Ultimate Goal:

Action Goals:

Tools and Routines:

Week _ Evaluation:

Aria 1 Trigger Words

Aria Title: _____

Write down six trigger words or phrases for each category. Then circle or underline the three that resonate most closely with what you want to communicate or execute.

Technical Trigger Words
-
-
-
-
-
-

Inner Awareness Trigger Words
-
-
-
-
-
-

Mental Muscle Trigger Words
-
-
-
-
-
-

Expressive Freedom Trigger Words
-
-
-
-
-
-

Aria 1 Trigger Words continued

Aria Title: _____

Finally, choose one trigger from each category, which captures the essence of your ultimate goal in that category. These are your final trigger words for this aria.

Technical:

Inner Awareness:

Mental Muscle:

Expressive Freedom:

Aria 2 Trigger Words

Aria Title: _____

Write down six trigger words or phrases for each category. Then circle or underline the three that resonate most closely with what you want to communicate or execute.

Technical Trigger Words
-
-
-
-
-
-

Inner Awareness Trigger Words
-
-
-
-
-
-

Mental Muscle Trigger Words
-
-
-
-
-
-

Expressive Freedom Trigger Words
-
-
-
-
-

Aria 2 Trigger Words continued

Aria Title: _____

Finally, choose one trigger from each category, which
captures the essence of your ultimate goal in that
category. These are your final trigger words for this
aria.

      Technical:

      Inner Awareness:

      Mental Muscle:

      Expressive Freedom:

Aria 3 Trigger Words

Aria Title: _____

Write down six trigger words or phrases for each category. Then circle or underline the three that resonate most closely with what you want to communicate or execute..

Technical Trigger Words
-
-
-
-
-
-

Inner Awareness Trigger Words
-
-
-
-
-
-

Mental Muscle Trigger Words

-
-
-
-
-
-

Expressive Freedom Trigger Words

-
-
-
-
-

Aria 3 Trigger Words continued

Aria Title: _____

Finally, choose one trigger from each category, which captures the essence of your ultimate goal in that category. These are your final trigger words for this aria.

Technical:

Inner Awareness:

Mental Muscle:

Expressive Freedom:

Aria 4 Trigger Words

Aria Title: _____

Write down six trigger words or phrases for each
category. Then circle or underline the three that resonate
most closely with what you want to communicate or
execute.

Technical Trigger Words
-
-
-
-
-
-

Inner Awareness Trigger Words
-
-
-
-
-
-

Mental Muscle Trigger Words
-
-
-
-
-
-

Expressive Freedom Trigger Words
-
-
-
-
-

Aria 4 Trigger Words continued

Aria Title: _____

Finally, choose one trigger from each category, which captures the essence of your ultimate goal in that category. These are your final trigger words for this aria.

Technical:

Inner Awareness:

Mental Muscle:

Expressive Freedom:

Creating A Personal Performance Environment and Character Analysis

Uta Hagen describes this exercise in her book, *Respect For Acting*, 1973. The version below has been adapted for singers.

Answer the following questions about five minutes out of a day in **your** life (today, yesterday, this week):

Who am I? (Full Name, Place of Birth, Physical Characteristics, Marital Status, Education Level, Social Status, Physical Condition, Grooming Habits, Style, Personality Traits)

What time is it? (Century, year, season, day, minute)

Creating A Personal Performance Environment and Character Analysis continued

Where am I? (Country, city, neighborhood, house, room, area of room, physical dimensions, doors or windows, outdoors, terrain, weather, temperature)

What does the space feel like? (Describe the atmosphere: Warm? Chilly? Stuffy? Dry? Describe the lighting. Describe the smells, background noises, visibility, what I see.)

What am I wearing? (Texture and color of fabric, fit, how it feels on my skin, how I move about or sit while wearing it)

Creating A Personal Performance Environment and Character Analysis continued

What surrounds me? (Animate and inanimate objects; am I alone or is someone else in my environment)

How do I feel in my environment? (What is my physical and emotional state?)

What are the given circumstances? (Past, present and future events influencing the circumstances)

Creating A Personal Performance Environment and Character Analysis continued

What is my relationship?   (My relationship to events, other people and things)

What do I want? (My main and immediate objectives)

What's in my way?   (Obstacles)

Creating A Personal Performance Environment and Character Analysis continued

What do I do to get what I want? (The action: physical, verbal)

Exercise 2:

Answer the same questions about **your character**, as he/she is about to sing the aria.

Who am I? (Character's Full Name, Place of Birth, Physical Characteristics, Marital Status, Education Level, Social Status, Physical Condition, Grooming Habits, Style, Personality Traits)

What time is it? (Century, year, season, day, minute)

Creating A Personal Performance Environment
and Character Analysis continued

Where am I? (Country, city, neighborhood, house, room, area of room, physical dimensions, doors or windows, outdoors, terrain, weather, temperature)

What does the space feel like? (Describe the atmosphere: Warm? Chilly? Stuffy? Dry? Describe the lighting. Describe the smells, background noises, visibility, what I see.)

What am I wearing? (Texture and color of fabric, fit, how it feels on my skin, how I move about or sit while wearing it)

What surrounds me? (Animate and inanimate objects, am I alone or is someone else in my environment)

Creating A Personal Performance Environment
and Character Analysis continued

How do I feel in my environment? (What is my
physical and emotional state?)

What are the given circumstances? (Past, present,
and future events influencing the circumstances)

What is my relationship? (To events, other people and
things)

What do I want? (What are my main and immediate
objectives)

Creating A Personal Performance Environment
and Character Analysis continued

What's in my way? (Obstacles)

What do I do to get what I want? (The action:
physical, verbal)

Performance Environment Trigger Words

You now have a sense of your circumstances before you sing the aria. This sense will contain all of the above information and will influence your physical and vocal choices as you begin to sing. Now try to think of trigger words or phrases that capture the essence of the situation your character is in. These words should immediately trigger the physical and emotional landscape of your character during the aria.

Aria 1:_____

_____

_____

_____

_____

Aria 2: _____

_____

_____

_____

_____

Performance Environment Trigger Words
continued

Aria 3: _____

_____

_____

_____

_____

_____

Aria 4: _____

_____

_____

_____

_____

_____

Mock Audition #1 Observations Worksheets

Write down your observations and impressions of your over all performance **before** listening to the recording. Recall what it felt like as you were singing the arias and describe how you perceived your performance in the moment you were singing. What went well? What did not go well?   Note any body tension, how well you concentrated, your ability to recover quickly in the case of mistakes, any negative self-talk or emotions that occurred. Note how successful you felt with the T-I-M-E elements you worked on this week.

Overall Performance Impressions:

Mock Audition #1 Observations Worksheets
continued

Aria 1_____

Technical

Inner Awareness

Mental Muscle

Expressive Freedom

Mock Audition #1 Observations Worksheets
continued

Aria 2_____

Technical

Inner Awareness

Mental Muscle

Expressive Freedom

Mock Audition #1 Observations Worksheets
continued

Aria 3_____

Technical

Inner Awareness

Mental Muscle

Expressive Freedom

Mock Audition #1 Observations Worksheets
continued

Aria 4_____

Technical

Inner Awareness

Mental Muscle

Expressive Freedom

Attitudes and Emotions Chart*

*Adapted from *Singing, Acting, and Movement in Opera*, Mark Cross, 2002

Alarmed	Amused	Angry	Annoyed	Apologetic	Arrogant
Ashamed	Awed	Bitter	Bold	Bored	Brazen
Breathless	Broken	Calculatin	Calm	Candid	Cautious
Cheerful	Cocky	Coquettish	Defiant	Dejected	Depressed
Desperate	Determined	Disoriented	Discouraged	Dumbfounded	Ecstatic
Elated	Elegant	Energetic	Enraged	Enraptured	Exhausted
Fearful	Feeble	Embarassed	Fidgety	Flirtatious	Forgiving
Frantic	Frightened	Furious	Gallant	Gentle	Giddy
Gracious	Graceful	Grumpy	Happy	Haughty	Helpless
Hopeful	Horrified	Humble	Humiliated	Hyper	Impatient
Impervious	Impish	Impulsive	Innocent	Introverted	Irksome
Irrerverent	Jaded	Jealous	Joking	Jolly	Joyful
Jubilant	Lazy	Lethargic	Lewd	Limp	Listless
Lively	Livid	Loving	Manic	Meek	Melancholic
Miserable	Mocking	Moody	Mournful	Naive	Naughty
Menacing	Needy	Nervous	Noble	Non-Chalant	Numb
Pathetic	Passive	Patronizing	Playful	Pleasant	Preoccupied
Pretentious	Proud	Rash	Reckless	Regal	Relaxed
Relieved	Resigned	Restless	Reverent	Sarcastic	Scornful
Sensitive	Serene	Serious	Shocked	Shameless	Sharp
Shy	Sincere	Solemn	Spiteful	Submissive	Sullen
Sulky	Sympathetic	Teasing	Tender	Tentative	Terrified
Thoughtful	Tough	Timid	Tired	Trusting	Troubled
Unbearable	Uncouth	Undecided	Understated	Uneasy	Worried

Feel free to add your own adjectives or adverbs.

Attitudes and Emotions Worksheets

Note: For this exercise, use different colored pens or pencils for each aria.

Using the Attitudes and Emotions Chart, identify and circle the main emotions driving your character throughout the aria. Next, list them below in the order of their importance.

Your Character's Emotional State and Attitude:

Aria 1_____

1._____

2._____

3._____

4._____

5_____

Attitudes and Emotions Worksheets continued

Describe in detail specific situations where you
have felt the same emotion or something similar.
What specifically triggered the emotion? As you
describe the triggering moment, can you feel the
emotion itself? Can you recall it vividly? Describe
what the emotion feels like in your body. Does it
trigger a certain physical response? ; tension?
quickened pulse?; tears?; a change in your
breathing pattern? Imagine watching yourself from
outside of your body. What do you look like?
What are your facial expressions for each emotion?
What is your body stance like?   Repeat this
exercise for each of the remaining arias.

Attitudes and Emotions Worksheets continued

Note: For this exercise, use different colored pens or pencils for each aria.

Using the Attitudes and Emotions Chart, identify and circle the main emotions driving your character throughout the aria. Next, list them below in the order of their importance.

Your Character's Emotional State and Attitude:

Aria 2_____

1._____

2._____

3._____

4._____

5_____

Attitudes and Emotions Worksheets continued

Describe in detail specific situations where you
have felt the same emotion or something similar.
What specifically triggered the emotion? As you
describe the triggering moment, can you feel the
emotion itself? Can you recall it vividly? Describe
what the emotion feels like in your body. Does it
trigger a certain physical response? ; tension?
quickened pulse?; tears?; a change in your
breathing pattern? Imagine watching yourself from
outside of your body. What do you look like?
What are your facial expressions for each emotion?
What is your body stance like? Repeat this
exercise for each of the remaining arias.

Attitudes and Emotions Worksheets continued

Note: For this exercise, use different colored pens
or pencils for each aria.

Using the Attitudes and Emotions Chart, identify
and circle the main emotions driving your character
throughout the aria. Next, list them below in the
order of their importance.

Your Character's Emotional State and Attitude:

Aria 3_____

1._____

2._____

3._____

4._____

5_____

Attitudes and Emotions Worksheets continued

Describe in detail specific situations where you
have felt the same emotion or something similar.
What specifically triggered the emotion? As you
describe the triggering moment, can you feel the
emotion itself? Can you recall it vividly? Describe
what the emotion feels like in your body. Does it
trigger a certain physical response? ; tension?
quickened pulse?; tears?; a change in your
breathing pattern? Imagine watching yourself from
outside of your body. What do you look like?
What are your facial expressions for each emotion?
What is your body stance like?   Repeat this
exercise for each of the remaining arias.

Attitudes and Emotions Worksheets continued

Note: For this exercise, use different colored pens or pencils for each aria.

Using the Attitudes and Emotions Chart, identify and circle the main emotions driving your character throughout the aria. Next, list them below in the order of their importance.

Your Character's Emotional State and Attitude:

Aria 4_____

1._____

2._____

3._____

4._____

5_____

Attitudes and Emotions Worksheets continued

Describe in detail specific situations where you
have felt the same emotion or something similar.
What specifically triggered the emotion? As you
describe the triggering moment, can you feel the
emotion itself? Can you recall it vividly? Describe
what the emotion feels like in your body. Does it
trigger a certain physical response? ; tension?
quickened pulse?; tears?; a change in your
breathing pattern? Imagine watching yourself from
outside of your body. What do you look like?
What are your facial expressions for each emotion?
What is your body stance like?   Repeat this
exercise for each of the remaining arias.

Triggering Sense Memory Worksheets

Using the answers you wrote to identify the emotions and attitudes of your character, identify the sensory elements:

Touch
Smell
Taste
Hearing
Sight

1. Identify all of the sensory elements that your character experiences immediately before, during and after the aria.
2. Recall your personal experience of each of the senses you described. Describe the sensations in detail. What did your body feel like leading up to the sense, in the center of the sense, as the sense wore off?

Ex. Bitter cold, no protection: Nose feels tingly and starts to run. Ears are like ice, hands balled up in fists and arms wrapped around the body to shut out wind. Forehead very cool, feet like ice blocks. Chin tucked into chest...

Try to recall what triggered the sense. Was it a cold wind against your face? Was it the sight of the snow-covered mountain where you took a walk? Was it the smell of the moist cold air?

Identify the trigger or stimulus for the sensation and you will be able to recall the emotion immediately and realistically.

Triggering Sense Memory Worksheets continued

Transfer the senses or stimuli for your senses to the situation you face in your aria. Experience the sense and the audience will experience it with you!

Character_____

My Personal Examples

Character_____

My Personal Examples

Triggering Sense Memory Worksheets continued

Character_____

My Personal Examples

Character_____

My Personal Examples

Aria Affirmations

Create five positive statements of fact in the present tense about what you do well in each of your audition arias.

Aria: _____

    1. _____

    2. _____

    3. _____

    4. _____

    5. _____

Aria: _____

    1. _____

    2. _____

    3. _____

    4. _____

    5. _____

Aria Affirmations continued

Aria: _____

    1. _____

    2. _____

    3. _____

    4. _____

    5. _____

Aria: _____

    1. _____

    2. _____

    3. _____

    4. _____

    5. _____

Mock #2 Audition Observations Worksheets

Write down your observations and impressions of
your over all performance **before** listening to the
recording. Recall what it felt like as you were
singing the arias and describe how you perceived
your performance in the moment you were singing.
What went well? What did not go well? Note any
body tension, how well you concentrated, your
ability to recover quickly in the case of mistakes,
any negative self-talk or emotions that occurred.
Note how successful you felt with the T-I-M-E
elements you worked on this week.

Overall Performance Impressions:

**Mock Audition #2 Observations Worksheets
continued**

Aria 1_____

Technical

Inner Awareness

Mental Muscle

Expressive Freedom

Mock Audition #2 Observations Worksheets
continued

Aria 2_____

Technical

Inner Awareness

Mental Muscle

Expressive Freedom

Mock Audition #2 Observations Worksheets
continued

Aria 3_____

Technical

Inner Awareness

Mental Muscle

Expressive Freedom

Mock Audition #2 Observations Worksheets
continued

Aria 4_____

Technical

Inner Awareness

Mental Muscle

Expressive Freedom

Adrenaline Scale Worksheet

Write how successful you were at bringing your excitement level under control so that you could perform optimally. Rate your experience on a scale of 1 (not successful) to 10 (very successful)

Aria 1_____

1   2   3   4   5   6   7   8   9   10

Comments:

Aria 2_____

1   2   3   4   5   6   7   8   9   10

Comments:

Adrenaline Scale Worksheet continued

Aria 3_____

1 2 3 4 5 6 7 8 9 10

Comments:

Aria 4_____

1 2 3 4 5 6 7 8 9 10

Comments:

Distractions Worksheet

List of distractions you will employ during practice:

1.

2.

3.

4.

5.

List any observations of your reaction to the various distractions and any strategies you think may help reduce the impact of distractions on your performance.

Creating Boundaries Worksheet

Your personal boundary is a protective apparatus that shields or protects you from all outside interference or distractions. Think of an image that offers you protection in moments of extreme danger. There are hundreds of possibilities: a circle of fire, a plastic bubble, a magic trick where you're able to beam up above it all or become invisible, a legion of angels standing guard. Experiment with the different images that come to mind.

Describe or draw the boundaries that come to your mind.

Magic Box Worksheet

Adapted from *Power Performance For Singers*, Alma
Thomas and Shirley Emmons, 1998

1. Sit quietly with your eyes closed and center
   yourself.
2. Imagine yourself sitting at a desk in front of
   a window.
3. Look out of the window and note what you
   see or hear around you.
4. On the desk is a sheet of blank paper, a pen
   and a box.
5. Pick up the pen and write down what is
   bothering you, what is distracting you and
   how it makes you feel. If you want, you can
   draw the distraction or your distracted
   mood.
6. Fold the piece of paper.
7. Look at the box on the desk. See the color,
   shape and size of the box. What is it made
   of? Open the lid and place the folded sheet
   of paper in the box and tell yourself you will
   deal with it later.
8. Go back to your practicing with the feeling
   of being free from the distraction.
9. Be sure to later go back to the imaginary
   room, desk and box. Open it and deal with
   the distraction. Give it the time it needs.
   Look at it from a distanced perspective.
   What do you need to do to overcome this
   distraction?
10. Often the distraction will have been resolved
    by just allowing yourself to not focus on it.

Ideal Performance Script Worksheet

This is a creative, visualizing exercise that helps you to actually describe your ideal performance as if your were writing a script that describes the actions of a character or perhaps your favorite performer. See yourself playing the role of the character you'ver written in the script. Write your Ideal Performance Script, describing in detail your performance day, arriving at the theater, who greets you back stage or at the stage door, what happens as you enter the stage, how you begin, what you feel as you start, how you sound and look as you sing, the audience reaction to you as well as those of your colleagues.

Afterwards, write a critique of your performance, as you would like to read it in the next day's newspaper.

Mock Audition #3 Observations Worksheets

Write down your observations and impressions of your over all performance **before** listening to the recording. Recall what it felt like as you were singing the arias and describe how you perceived your performance in the moment you were singing. What went well? What did not go well? Note any body tension, how well you concentrated, your ability to recover quickly in the case of mistakes, any negative self-talk or emotions that occurred. Note how successful you felt with the T-I-M-E elements you worked on this week.

Overall Performance Impressions:

Mock Audition #3 Observations Worksheets
continued

Aria 1_____

Technical

Inner Awareness

Mental Muscle

Expressive Freedom

**Mock Audition #3 Observations Worksheets
continued**

Aria 2 _____

Technical

Inner Awareness

Mental Muscle

Expressive Freedom

Mock Audition #3 Observations Worksheets
continued

Aria 3_____

Technical

Inner Awareness

Mental Muscle

Expressive Freedom

Mock Audition #3 Observations Worksheets
continued

Aria 4_____

Technical

Inner Awareness

Mental Muscle

Expressive Freedom

My Audition Day Intention Statement

Center yourself, form your intention to nail your audition and write it down.

Daily Routine Log

Day 7
Breakfast
Time:

Contents:

Lunch
Time:

Contents:

Dinner
Time:

Contents

Snacks:

Hours of sleep (incl. Naps)

Comments:

Daily Routine Log Continued

Day 6
Breakfast
Time:

Contents:

Lunch
Time:

Contents:

Dinner
Time:

Contents

Snacks:

Hours of sleep (incl. Naps)

Comments:

Daily Routine Log Continued

Day 5
Breakfast
Time:

Contents:

Lunch
Time:

Contents:

Dinner
Time:

Contents

Snacks:

Hours of sleep (incl. Naps)

Comments:

Daily Routine Log Continued

Day 4
Breakfast
Time:

Contents:

Lunch
Time:

Contents:

Dinner
Time:

Contents

Snacks:

Hours of sleep (incl. Naps)

Comments:

Daily Routine Log Continued

Day 3
Breakfast
Time:

Contents:

Lunch
Time:

Contents:

Dinner
Time:

Contents

Snacks:

Hours of sleep (incl. Naps)

Comments:

Daily Routine Log Continued

Day 2
Breakfast
Time:

Contents:

Lunch
Time:

Contents:

Dinner
Time:

Contents

Snacks:

Hours of sleep (incl. Naps)

Comments:

Audition Needs List

List everything you will need to prepare for your audition. Include your audition wardrobe, music for the pianist, your ECP, etc.)

List of what you will need to take with you to the audition (water, extra pantyhose, snack, music, affirmations, trigger words, ECP, etc.)

Emergency Contingency Plans (ECP)

Prepare for any crisis that could occur beforehand. What are your emergency warm-up exercises, positive affirmations, trigger words, adrenaline curbing or pumping exercises, distraction reminders, etc.? Remember, to win any battle, you need a good PLAN!

The Do's and Don'ts of the Audition Wardrobe

An audition is the closest singers get to the traditional "interview" experience. The first thing you present of yourself, before you sing a note, is your appearance. This seems obvious, but I've often been shocked and appalled to see the many ill-advised choices made by singers. Keeping in mind that the European standard is much more relaxed, I still prefer the safer, more conservative or universal approach.

A good question to pose for yourself is this: "Keeping in mind the roles I am competing for, does what I am wearing compliment or distract from my overall appearance and my singing?"

MEN

- *Do make sure that your clothes fit properly.*
- *Do wear a sports jacket (suits and ties are optional) with either a dress shirt or solid colored sweater or turtleneck.*
- *Do make sure your clothes are properly groomed (clean and ironed).*
- *Do wear dress shoes or boots.*
- *Do make sure your shoes or boots are polished.*
- *Do wear colors that match or complement each other.*
- *Do make sure your hair is washed and groomed.*
- *Do make sure your facial hair (mustache or beard) is groomed.*

The Do's and Don'ts of the Audition Wardrobe
continued

Men continued:

> ➢ *Do make sure you are personally groomed (take a shower, use deodorant, clip your fingernails, etc.)*
> ➢ *Do carry a handkerchief with you if you are prone to sweating.*
> ➢ *Do not wear bold prints*
> ➢ *Do not wear t-shirts (designer t-shirts included), unless under a sports jacket.*
> ➢ *Do not wear jeans (designer jeans included).*
> ➢ *Do not wear sports shoes of any kind (no thick rubber soles, please).*

WOMEN

> ➢ *Do wear a skirt or dress, unless you are specifically auditioning for a trouser role. If you simply must wear pants, wear a pantsuit of one solid color.*
> ➢ *Do make sure the skirt or dress is within close proximity to your knees (no mini skirts please).*
> ➢ *Do wear solid colors or minimal prints (trimming on a sweater or shirt, for example).*
> ➢ *Do make sure your clothes fit properly (not too tight or too baggy) and accentuate your figure (no fleshy arms, rolls or bulges hanging about).*
> ➢ *Do wear the proper undergarments to avoid lines, rolls, or bulges.*

The Do's and Don'ts of the Audition Wardrobe
continued

Women continued:

➤ *Do wear colors that complement your complexion*

➤ *Do wear cuts and fabrics that complement your figure.*

➤ *If you are overweight, avoid clining fabrics like jersey or lycra, and prints.).*

➤ *Do wear closed-toe dress shoes (no sandals please).*

➤ *Do wear shoes with a heel, even a small one (flat shoes with skirts/dresses on stage are unflattering).*

➤ *Do make sure your shoes and clothes are properly polished and ironed.*

➤ *Do wear make-up, but not too much (stage lights wash out your features and make-up can even out your complexion).*

➤ *Do consult a professional make-up artist (many department stores have specialists who can advise you).*

➤ *Do consult a professional hair stylist about the proper style and cut for your face.*

➤ *Do make sure your hair is groomed (washed, styled).*

➤ *Do not wear bangs. (Bangs create a shadow over your face under stage lights and take the focus away from your eyes.)*

➤ *Do not wear glitter, sequins or rhinestones.*

➤ *Do not wear evening clothes.*

➤ *Do not wear too much jewelry.*

➤ *Do not wear sleeveless or strapless dresses or tops.*

➤ *Do not wear jeans or tee shirts.*

Goals Assessment Worksheets

List all the improvements made toward reaching
your ultimate goal. Rate on a scale of 1 to 10, your
consistency in singing the aria at a "performance
ready" level in performance mode. (1 equals 10% of
the time and 10 equals 100% of the time)

Aria_____

Scale of performance ready consistency:

1   2   3   4   5   6   7   8   9   10

Aria_____

Scale of performance ready consistency:

1   2   3   4   5   6   7   8   9   10

Goals Assessment Worksheets continued

Aria_____

Scale of performance ready consistency:

1   2   3   4   5   6   7   8   9   10

Aria_____

Scale of performance ready consistency:

1   2   3   4   5   6   7   8   9   10

Final Affirmations Worksheet

Based on the evidence seen and heard from your recordings, feedback and personal observations make a final list of performance affirmations for your audition arias. Include in your statements the goals you've reached and the improvements you've made. Remember to write your positive statements in the present tense.

1.

2.

3.

4.

5.

6.

7.

8.

9.

10.

Final Aria Trigger Words

Based on your work over the past weeks, choose
one trigger word or phrase for each aria that puts
you in the musical, emotional and physical
landscape of your character. It should be a word or
phrase that "takes you there" immediately.

Aria_____

Trigger:

Aria_____

Trigger:

Aria_____

Trigger:

Aria_____

Trigger:

Audition Evaluation Worksheets

Describe your overall impressions about the entire audition experience. Were you happy with your overall performance? Did you perform as well as you did during your mock auditions?   Were you able to remain focused, create your performance environment, and use your adrenaline positively? Did you remember why you sing? Were you able to communicate that confidently? Recall each and every success even if it wasn't consistently the case.

Audition Evaluation Worksheets continued

In the 2 columns below, write what went well and what didn't. Write down what you think would help you to improve what didn't go as well as you would have liked. Now, cross out the negatives of your experience. Save the positive comments for later reflection prior to your next audition. For some reason we tend to forget the positive, but we have no problems remembering the negative.

Repeat this evaluation for each audition you sing.

Positives	Negatives

About the Author

American Soprano Janet Williams has won critical acclaim for performances in leading roles at the Metropolitan Opera, Berlin Staatsoper, Paris Opera, Opera de Lyon, Nice Opera, Geneva Opera, Frankfurt Opera, Cologne Opera, Leipzig Opera, Théâtre Royal de la Monnaie, San Francisco Opera, Washington Opera, Dallas Opera and Michigan Opera Theatre, as well as in concerts throughout Europe, North America, Canada, Israel and Japan with conductors including Vladimir Ashkenazy, Daniel Barenboim, René Jacobs, Sir Neville Marriner, Zubin Mehta, Kent Nagano, Donald Runnicles and Michael Tilson Thomas.   Her recordings include Handel's *Messiah* with Nicholas McGegan and the Philharmonia Baroque Orchestra, Brahms' *Ein Deutsches Requiem* with Daniel Barenboim and the Chicago Symphony, and Graun's *Cleopatra e Cesare* with René Jacobs and Concerto Köln.

Janet Williams' repertoire spans genres of musical styles from Baroque to Contemporary in the lyric-coloratura *fach*. She has coached with some of the most respected singers and teachers of our times, including Camilla Williams, Reri Grist, Helen Donath, Marilyn Horne, Regine Crespin, Mirella Freni, and Vocal Pedagogue David Jones. She holds a Master of Music Degree in Vocal Performance from Indiana University. Janet Williams is Director of *Performance Enhancement by Design*, which offers a variety of master classes, workshops, and seminars throughout Europe and the United States. She lives in Berlin with her husband, stage director and set designer Fred Berndt.